English Language Toolbox

Proverbs

Betty Kirkpatrick MA

First published 2003 by **Learners Publishing Pte Ltd**
222 Tagore Lane, #03–01 TG Building, Singapore 787603

Reprinted 2003, 2004

Email: learnpub@learners.com.sg
Visit our website: http://www.learners.com.sg

ISBN 981 4107 15 8

Printed by COS Printers Pte Ltd, Singapore

ASSOCIATE COMPANIES

RIC Learners International Limited
PO Box 332
Greenwood
Western Australia 6924

RIC Publications Limited (Asia)
5th floor, Gotanda Mikado Building
2-5-8 Hiratsuka
Shinagawa-ku Tokyo
JAPAN 142-0051
Tel: 03-3788-9201
Fax: 03-3788 9202
Email: elt@ricpublications.com
Website: www.ricpublications.com

Learners Educational Publishing Sdn Bhd
43A, Jalan 34/154, Taman Delima
56000 Cheras, Kuala Lumpur, Malaysia
Tel: 603-9100-1868
Fax: 603-9102-4730
Email: enquiry@learners.com.my

CONTENTS

PREFACE

Proverbs are an important part of the English language, many of them having been in the language for several hundreds of years. They are traditional sayings which take the form of concise sentences and they are usually expressed in clever, witty or memorable language. In content, they tend to offer advice or make some kind of moral comment on how we should lead our lives.

Of the many hundreds of proverbs in the English language, a surprising number of them are still in common use. This book contains a selection of these, arranging them alphabetically according to the first word in the proverb. Each proverb, listed in bold type, has been given a short explanation followed by two or three example sentences, in italic type, to illustrate how it is used. Common variants or shortened forms have also been given in bold where these exist, and a note has been added on the origin of the proverb, where this is relevant. Proverbs which are similar in meaning, or opposite in meaning, to the proverb being explained, are in the margin next to the explanation. Thus, at **Absence makes the heart grow fonder**, **Distance lends enchantment to the view** has been given as a proverb which is similar in meaning and **Out of**

sight, out of mind has been given as one which is opposite in meaning.

Categories in the English language are rarely clear-cut and they have a habit of merging into each other. So it is that some proverbs have become cliché, because they are so widely use, and this has been mentioned in the explanation. So it is, also, that the main part of some proverbs also functions as an idiom. For example, **Don't count your chickens before they are hatched** is a common proverb and the idiomatic phrase **count your chickens** is also commonly used. Where this is the case, it has been indicated in the text.

In addition to the proverb entries, the book contains a series of passages which indicate how proverbs are actually used in a piece of text. This enhances the information given by the example sentences.

A set of exercises, with accompanying answers, has also been included in the book so that students can test their comprehension of the material which the book provides. Proverbs add interest and colour to the English language and a knowledge of them will enrich both the learner's comprehension and use of English.

Betty Kirkpatrick

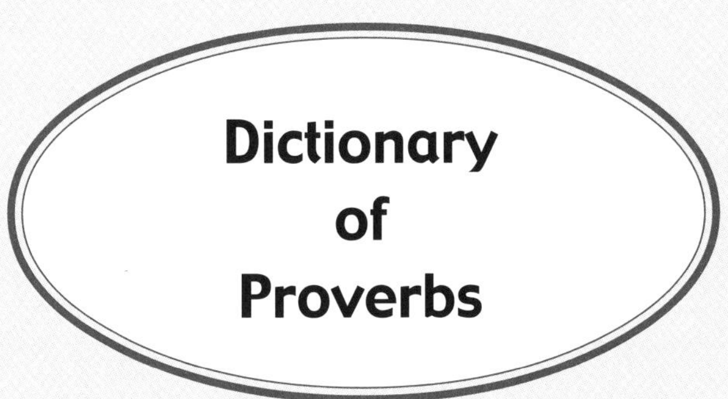
Dictionary
of
Proverbs

A

A bird in the hand is worth two in the bush

It is better to hold on to something which you already have, than to try to get something less attainable; you might not succeed in getting it and you might even risk losing what you have: ♦ *Jack went for several interviews and has already been offered a job which he has either to accept or reject right away. He really has to decide whether* ***a bird in the hand is worth two in the bush****, because he is still waiting to hear about a job with much better prospects.* ♦ *We've decided to rent this flat, even though it's not exactly what we're looking for and we still have some more to go and look at. Flats to rent are scarce in this area and we've decided that* ***a bird in the hand is worth two in the bush****.*

Similar

It is best to be on the safe side.

Help

This proverb is frequently found in the shortened form **a bird in the hand**, which has become a cliché:

♦ *Beth's brother advised her not to take the first teaching post she was offered, but to take time to see what was available. However, she went against his advice and accepted the offer; she needed money right away and it was a case of* ***a bird in the hand****.*

A burnt child dreads the fire

A person who has a bad experience concerning something will avoid it in future: ♦ *Jill says that she was so unhappy when she was married that she will never marry again;* ***a burnt child dreads the fire****, I suppose.* ♦ *Mary had such a bad time giving birth to her daughter that she says that she is not going to have any more children. She may change her mind, but it could be the case that* ***a burnt child dreads the fire****.* ♦ ***A burnt child dreads the fire*** *and Sue's already had a bad experience from buying a second-hand car. This time she says that she's buying a brand-new one.*

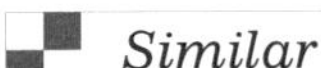
Similar

Once bitten, twice shy.

A cat may look at a king

There is no reason why an ordinary or humble person should not look at someone of great importance. This proverb is used to emphasize equality of people and often said when someone is accused of staring at someone else: ♦ *'Why are you staring at me?' the beautiful young woman asked the rather shabby young man on the bus. 'I wasn't staring,' he replied, 'and **a cat may look at a king**.'* ♦ *The child was looking in wonder at the jewels which the old lady was wearing. When the old lady pushed him aside haughtily, the child's mother said angrily, '**A cat may look at a king**.'*

A change is as good as a rest

Similar

Variety is the spice of life.

A change from your usual routine will do you as much good as a holiday from it: ♦ *I'm surprised that Jane doesn't get tired, because she teaches PE during term time and then has a job as a tennis coach all summer. She claims that **a change is as good as a rest**.* ♦ *Mum says that **a change is as good as a rest**, and that she doesn't mind taking a self-catering holiday place where she'll end up doing most of the shopping and cooking.* ♦ *Bob was a policeman until he reached retirement age and now he's got a job as a security guard when he could be taking life easy. However, he says that, for him, **a change is as good as a rest**.*

A drowning man will clutch at a straw

Similar

Hope springs eternal.

While there's life, there's hope.

In a desperate situation a person will grab at the slightest possibility of assistance, even though this attempt is likely to be futile: ♦ *Peter has completely failed to find anywhere to live and, as a last resort, has asked Mark to put him up, even though he and Mark have disliked each other for years. It's obvious that Mark will refuse, but **a drowning man will clutch at a straw**.* ♦ *George has massive debts, the bank has refused to* *extend his overdraft and his parents will not lend him any more money.* ***A drowning man will clutch at a straw****, however; he's now thinking of asking his ex-wife for a loan, although he treated her very badly and she won't even speak to him.* ♦ *Jane has been told by two cancer specialists that her husband's condition is terminal, but she refuses to accept this and has made an appointment for him to see another doctor;* ***a drowning man will clutch at a straw****.*

Help

The phrase **clutch at straws** is also commonly used to mean to take desperate, probably futile, action:

♦ *I think you're* ***clutching at straws*** *by phoning the restaurant to find out if you left your purse there; I'm sure that you had it in the taxi on the way home.* ♦ *The doctor said that to subject the patient to the new treatment would be to* ***clutch at straws*** *and that the treatment would cause him great discomfort.*

A fool and his money are soon parted

If you don't take good care of your money and use it sensibly, you will soon lose it. This proverb is used to indicate that someone is being cheated or taken advantage of financially by someone else, or that someone has paid too much for something: ♦ *Tony must be mad to invest any money in Nick's company because everyone knows that it will fail; still, I suppose* ***a fool and his money are soon parted****.* ♦ *The new owner of that house paid far more than it is worth; still, it seems that he is very wealthy and* ***a fool and his money are soon parted****.* ♦ *When Lucy married a wealthy businessman she gave up work and now she's bored and spends a great deal of money on clothes which she doesn't need and hardly ever wears;* ***a fool and his money are soon parted****.*

A friend in need is a friend indeed

A true friend is someone who helps you when you are in some kind of difficulty or trouble: ♦ *When my flat was badly damaged in the fire, Jenny immediately invited me to stay with her until I could get into my flat again;* ***a friend in need is a friend indeed****.* ♦ *Even his own family were reluctant to lend Pete money to pay off his debts, although he is known to be a very honest person. But Johnny had no hesitation in doing so;* ***a friend in need is a friend indeed****.* ♦ *Our car broke down and we would never have got to the airport, which is several miles away, had Anna not offered to take us there, even though it was late at night and foggy;* ***a friend in need is a friend indeed****.*

Help

The same idea is conveyed by the saying **it's at times like these you know who your friends are**:

♦ *Jean and her three children were left homeless when she couldn't pay the rent on her flat and only Sally offered to help;* ***it's at times like these you know who your friends are****.*

A golden key can open any door

Similar

Every man has his price.

Money talks.

Money is power.

Opposite

Money isn't everything.

This proverb is used to emphasize the great power and influence which the possession of wealth brings: ♦ *Pam failed to get into the college of her choice and then we heard that she had suddenly got a place there. Most people suspect that it had something to do with the fact that her wealthy father had given the college a huge contribution towards a new sports stadium; this seems like proof that* ***a golden key can open any door****.* ♦ *There's a shortage of well-qualified workers in this area and we're quite a small company. Our larger and wealthier competitors don't have quite such a problem because* ***a golden key can open any door****.* ♦ *It's difficult to get a visa to visit that country at such short notice and Mark only succeeded in getting one because his father is a wealthy diplomat;* ***a golden key can open any door****.*

A good beginning makes a good ending

If a job or project is carried out properly from the start, with enough attention being given to preparation and planning, then it is likely to turn out well: ♦ *If you're going to redecorate the house yourself, you should make sure that you prepare all the surfaces properly;* ***a good beginning makes a good ending****.* ♦ *It's important for young couples to spend a lot of time with each other and to get to know each other really well before they get married;* ***a good beginning makes a good ending****.* ♦ *It's only August and we're holding the first meeting of the organizing committee for the Christmas charity fair. This is because, from the experience of previous years, we know that spending a lot of time on planning and preparation makes for a much more successful occasion and much more money for charity;* ***a good beginning makes a good ending****.*

Similar

Well begun is half done.

It is the first step that is difficult.

A house divided cannot stand

Unity is important if an organization is going to succeed: ♦ *It is important that the prime minister has the backing of all the cabinet ministers on this issue;* ***a house divided cannot stand****.* ♦ *We need complete loyalty and commitment from all supporters if our candidate is to win the election;* ***a house divided cannot stand****.* ♦ *There was so much infighting within the organization that the charity was making very little money and so was wound up;* ***a house divided cannot stand****.*

Similar

United we stand, divided we fall.

Union is strength.

Did you know?

The original version of this proverb was **a house divided against itself cannot stand** and this is a biblical allusion, being a reference to Mark 3:25—'If a house be divided against itself, that house cannot stand.'

A liar ought to have a good memory

It is important that liars have good memories so that they will be able to remember what lies they told and not contradict themselves: ♦ ***A liar ought to have a good memory****; Lisa told me yesterday that she couldn't go to the cinema with me in the evening because she was looking after her sister's children; today, however, she told me that she had gone out for a meal with Frank last night.* ♦ *Jim went to a football match yesterday afternoon instead of being at work, but told the boss that he was going to a funeral.* ***A liar ought to have a good memory*** *because today Jim told the boss that he had had a hospital appointment yesterday afternoon.* ♦ ***A liar ought to have a good memory****; the councillor told one of our committee members that he had not been able to attend the protest meeting because he was going to be out of town on business, but he told another member that his absence was because of illness.*

Help

The proverb also exists in the form of **a liar needs a good memory**.

A little knowledge is a dangerous thing

Having a slight knowledge and understanding of something can lead to problems, especially if you overestimate your knowledge and try to deal with something which requires much greater knowledge: ♦ *Jack says that he knows enough about building to carry out the repairs to the house himself. But* ***a little knowledge is a dangerous thing****; I think he will get into difficulties very quickly and have to call in a qualified tradesman.* ♦ *Anne had taken a first-aid course and suggested that she tried to help the injured cyclist while we waited for the ambulance to arrive. However, we could see that he was very badly hurt and advised her not to touch him;* ***a little knowledge is a dangerous thing****.* ♦ *Jane says that she has read the instruction manual and* *feels that she can repair the washing machine herself. Nevertheless, her flatmates have pointed out that* ***a little knowledge is a dangerous thing*** *and are insisting on sending for an engineer.*

Help

The earlier form of the proverb is **a little learning is a dangerous thing**, a quotation from Alexander Pope's *Essay on Criticism* (1711), and it is also still current. In its later form, the proverb has become a cliché.

A man is known by the company he keeps

People tend to assume that, in character, you will be very similar to your friends and those with whom you choose to associate: ♦ ***A man is known by the company he keeps****; if you go around with that gang of rowdy youths too much, people will think that you are just like them.* ♦ *Jill's parents disapproved of her new boyfriend even before they met him. He's a close friend of their next-door neighbour's rather nasty son and they firmly believe that* ***a man is known by the company he keeps****.* ♦ *Jim is a quiet, responsible person, but he goes to football matches with some people who got into trouble with the police and his new neighbours are worried in case he's just like his friends;* ***a man is known by the company he keeps****.*

Similar

Birds of a feather flock together.

Like will to like.

A miss is as good as a mile

If someone has failed to do something, or if someone or something has missed someone or something else, it does not matter whether they have failed or missed by a small or large amount; the effect is still the same: ♦ *The bullet missed James by a few centimetres, but he was very brave about his narrow escape, saying, '****A miss is as good as a mile****.'* ♦ *The other car nearly hit mine head-on. Although I tried telling myself that* ***a miss is as good as a mile****, I had nightmares* *about the near accident for several months.* ♦ *It is true that our team lost the championship by only one point, but* ***a miss is as good as a mile****.*

Help

The modern version of the proverb is a shortened form of **an inch in a miss is as good as an ell**, which makes more sense. An ell was a former measure of length equal to just over a mile.

A new broom sweeps clean

A person who is appointed to a new job will make major changes, whether these are necessary or not: ♦ *The new manager is bound to want to get rid of some of the office staff and appoint people chosen by him;* ***a new broom sweeps clean****.* ♦ *The present system of recording sales works very well, but the new sales manager is insisting on changing it all; it's very annoying, but* ***a new broom sweeps clean****.* ♦ ***A new broom sweeps clean*** *and the new head of the department has already made several criticisms about how things are done; it's made us all very nervous.*

Help

The expression **new broom**, meaning someone recently appointed who is likely to make changes, is also common and has become a cliché:

♦ *The new manager is rather a* ***new broom*** *and we're worried that he may want to make staff changes.* ♦ *Workers were worried enough about their jobs without the arrival of the* ***new broom*** *in the boardroom.*

Did you know?

In origin, the proverb refers to an early form of broom which was made of twigs strapped to a long handle. The broom was much more effective when the twigs were freshly cut.

A nod is as good as a wink to a blind horse

A slight sign or hint is all that is necessary to get someone to understand what you mean in a particular situation: ♦ *My mother just had to raise an eyebrow and I realized that she didn't believe me;* ***a nod is as good as a wink to a blind horse****.* ♦ *Jane opened her book and I understood immediately that she wanted to be left alone;* ***a nod is as good as a wink to a blind horse****.* ♦ *Sara looked at her watch and we knew that she was annoyed at our late arrival;* ***a nod is as good as a wink to a blind horse****.*

Help

This proverb is sometimes shortened to **a nod is as good as a wink**:

♦ *Our host collected all the plates and glasses and went into the kitchen;* ***a nod's as good as a wink*** *and we realized that it was time to leave.*

A penny saved is a penny earned

If you save a penny, it is as if you have earned it again, because you will still have a penny; if you spend it, you will have nothing: ♦ *Ron is very thrifty and saves most of his salary; his motto is '****A penny saved is a penny earned****'.* ♦ *All his life Mr Watson has firmly believed that* ***a penny saved is a penny earned*** *and is now very wealthy. Still, it would have been better if he had spent some of his money on enjoying himself; he is now a lonely old man with no close relatives.* ♦ *It is difficult to persuade today's young people that* ***a penny saved is a penny earned****, because we live in a very commercial world where they are encouraged to spend, spend, spend.*

A place for everything, and everything in its place

This proverb recommends orderliness and is particularly liked by extremely tidy people: ♦ *Aunt*

Martha's house is always incredibly neat and tidy; '**A place for everything, and everything in its place**' *is her motto.* ♦ *Rob said that he couldn't possibly live at the house of his girlfriend's parents. Her mother tidies things away as soon as he puts them down, and practically drives him mad by always saying,* '**A place for everything, and everything in its place**.' ♦ *Apparently, Sally and Jane are thinking about sharing a flat together, but I can't see that arrangement working out. Sally is incredibly untidy and, as far as Jane is concerned, it is a case of* **a place for everything, and everything in its place**.

A prophet is not without honour, save in his own country

Someone's ability or talent is not always recognized or acknowledged by their fellow countrymen or by those who are close to them, although they may be held in high regard elsewhere: ♦ *We have several authors who are far better known abroad than they are here;* **a prophet is not without honour, save in his own country**. ♦ *The scientist was the most important person ever to be born in that town, but no one there ever paid the slightest attention to him;* **a prophet is not without honour, save in his own country**. ♦ **A prophet is not without honour, save in his own country**; *Molly is becoming very well known as a violinist and regularly plays in the most prestigious international orchestras, but no one in her home village is even aware that she plays a musical instrument.*

Help

The proverb is not always used in its full form. It is often shortened to the less formal **a prophet in his own country**:

♦ *Professor Brown's research has been greatly applauded in the American journals, but has received little comment here; a case of* **a prophet in his own country**, *it seems.*

Did you know?

The proverb is biblical in origin. It is a reference to Matthew 13:57—'A prophet is not without honour, save in his own country, and in his own house.' This was the reply of Jesus to the attitude of the people of Nazareth when he returned to his home town to spread his teachings and practise healing. They treated him with disrespect and cynicism because he was just the son of the local carpenter.

A rolling stone gathers no moss

This proverb recommends stability and settling down; someone who is constantly moving from place to place and never settles down does not acquire money and possessions: ♦ *Jim's two brothers went to work in the family firm as young men and are now affluent businessmen. Jim, however, has spent a lifetime travelling and changing jobs and is now very badly off;* ***a rolling stone gathers no moss****.* ♦ *Most of Jackie's university friends now have good jobs and have a very comfortable lifestyle. But she hasn't yet decided what she wants to do and goes from temporary job to temporary job without earning very much;* ***a rolling stone gathers no moss****.* ♦ *Fred has travelled the world and his nephews love to hear about his adventures and think he's had a wonderful life. Nevertheless,* ***a rolling stone gathers no moss*** *and Fred is now virtually penniless, living on state benefit.*

Help

The phrase **a rolling stone** is also commonly used and has become a cliché:

♦ *The manager was impressed with Alice's work, when she had a temporary job here in the summer, and offered her a permanent job at a good salary. But Alice is* ***a rolling stone*** *and she turned the offer down.* ♦ *Jack has been* ***a rolling stone*** *all his life and we never thought that he would settle down. Yet as soon as he met Jill he became a changed person and now has a permanent job and a mortgage.*

Did you know?

The proverb dates from early times when most people lived and worked in settled agricultural communities and did not move around very much. Those who did were considered to be feckless and not able to hold down a job. Nowadays, the attitude to moving has changed, with many people moving from job to job to gain promotion and so earn more money, unlike the original rolling stone. The original form of the proverb was **the rolling stone gathers no seaweed** but the present version has been around at least since the sixteenth century.

A rose by any other name would smell as sweet

The proverb emphasizes how unimportant what name is given to a person or thing; it's what a person or thing is that is important: ♦ *I just need someone who will look after my children carefully and lovingly and I don't care whether you call her a nanny or children's nurse;* ***a rose by any other name would smell as sweet****.* ♦ *My American friend asked me to have a good vacation and my British friend told me to have a good holiday. I don't mind what they call it as long as I get a break from work;* ***a rose by any other name would smell as sweet****.* ♦ *Joan and Mike are planning to open a small eating establishment in the town. But they're not sure whether to call it a restaurant or whether to call it a bistro, or even a brasserie. But it really doesn't matter as long as the food is good;* ***a rose by any other name would smell as sweet****.*

Help

This is a very common proverb and often appears in the shortened form **a rose by any other name**:

♦ *Mike has started to call his secretary his personal assistant, but she does exactly the same job as before;* ***a rose by any other name****.*

The proverb comes from a passage in Shakespeare's play *Romeo and Juliet*: 'What's in a name? that which we call a rose by any other name would smell as sweet.'

A stitch in time saves nine

If you do something about a problem right away, you will prevent it from getting any worse and so save yourself time and effort: ♦ *We should get the roof repaired right away when there is only one slate missing;* ***a stitch in time saves nine*** *and we don't want to be faced with a huge roof bill later.* ♦ *One of the rose bushes is diseased and I must deal with it right away;* ***a stitch in time saves nine*** *and I don't want it to spread to the other rose bushes.* ♦ *The car's engine is making an odd noise and I'm going to take it to the workshop to get it checked out;* ***a stitch in time saves nine****.*

Similar

Prevention is better than cure.

Help

If you mend a piece of clothing as soon as a small hole appears, it will prevent the hole from becoming bigger and requiring more drastic mending.

A trouble shared is a trouble halved

It often helps to discuss a problem with someone, rather than worry about it alone: ♦ *I felt better after I had discussed my work problems with my husband;* ***a trouble shared is a trouble halved*** *and he gave me some good advice.* ♦ *You should mention your health worries to Meg;* ***a trouble shared is a trouble halved****, and, in any case, she is a trained nurse.* ♦ *Discussing my money problems with Jenny seemed to make them less serious than I had feared; it's true that* ***a trouble shared is a trouble halved****.*

A watched pot never boils

When you are waiting for something to happen, it does not happen any sooner; indeed, it seems to take longer to happen if you keep checking: ♦ *Stop looking out of the window to see if the postman is coming yet;* ***a watched pot never boils****.* ♦ *The children planted some seeds in a window box and looked at least twice a day to see if the shoots were coming through, only to be* *disappointed; it was a case of* **a watched pot never boils**. ♦ *I know you are excited about your fiancé's arrival, but the train isn't due for half an hour more and so there's no point in standing on the platform;* **a watched pot never boils**.

Help

The proverb is frequently found in the shortened form **a watched pot**:

♦ *The children kept going to see if the hens had laid any eggs yet, but it was a case of* **a watched pot**.

Absence makes the heart grow fonder

Similar

Distance lends enchantment to the view.

Opposite

Out of sight, out of mind.

Feelings of affection for someone or something become stronger when they are not with you: ♦ *Mary never pays much attention to her little brother, but he has been away from home for a month and she's really looking forward to his return; clearly,* **absence makes the heart grow fonder**. ♦ *John and his fiancée, Sara, seem to be very happy, although they live several hundreds of miles from each other and only see each other every second weekend; perhaps* **absence makes the heart grow fonder**. ♦ *When Jim was working in this office, he said that it was a very boring place to work, but now he says he misses it very much;* **absence makes the heart grow fonder**.

Did you know?

The theory behind the expression is that you tend to remember only the good things about people when they are not there to keep reminding you of their faults.

Accidents will happen

Things are likely to go wrong unexpectedly at some stage in everyone's life, however careful people are. The proverb is often used to excuse or minimize an accidental misfortune which has occurred: ♦ *Liz takes care of her children very well, but her toddler pulled a cup of hot tea from the table all over himself. She was extremely upset, even though we kept telling her that* ***accidents will happen****.* ♦ *Bill is a very experienced joiner, but he cut his hand badly with a saw last week;* ***accidents will happen****.* ♦ *It's most unfortunate that Pam tripped over the dog and broke her ankle, but* ***accidents will happen****.*

Help

The proverb was originally common in the slightly longer form of **accidents will happen in the best-regulated families**:

♦ *We all try to protect our children from injury as much as possible, but, inevitably, some of them break limbs at some stage in their lives;* ***accidents will happen in the best-regulated families****.*

An alternative form of this proverb is **accidents do happen**.

Actions speak louder than words

What you do is more important than what you say: ♦ *The politician is always talking about what his party will do, but they never seem to do anything. Someone should tell him that* ***actions speak louder than words****.* ♦ *All the members of the family claim to love their grandmother very much, but Sue is the only one who pays her regular visits; the others should remember that* ***actions speak louder than words****.* ♦ *Bill frequently talks about the plight of the homeless, but he refused to make a donation to a charity which supports them; he should be aware that* ***actions speak louder than words****.*

Similar

Fine words butter no parsnips.

After a storm comes a calm

After a period of trouble or unrest, a period of peace will come. This proverb is often used to give hope to someone who is experiencing a period of trouble and to remind them that things will improve: ♦ *For a few months, there were regular border skirmishes, but they stopped after both sides agreed to sign a truce;* ***after a storm comes a calm****.* ♦ *For several days Jane*

Similar

The darkest hour is just before the dawn.

and Peter were both very angry and kept screaming at each other, but then they stopped quarrelling and became friends again; it was a case of ***after a storm comes a calm****.*

All good things must come to an end

Similar

Everything has an end.

All enjoyable things have to end some time. The proverb is often used when someone is reluctant to leave something which they have been enjoying very much: ♦ *The children were sad on the last day of the holiday and we explained gently to them that* ***all good things must come to an end****.* ♦ *It's been a very enjoyable party, but* ***all good things must come to an end*** *and it's time to go home now.* ♦ *We had a lovely time at the seaside and wished that we could have stayed longer, but* ***all good things must come to an end****.*

Help

The proverb is now so commonly used that it has become a cliché. It originally took the form **all things come to an end**.

All is grist that comes to the (someone's) mill

Everything or every experience, situation, etc, can be used to the advantage or profit of someone: ♦ *You no longer have to be a member of the club to eat in the restaurant;* ***all is grist that comes to our mill****.* ♦ *The politician has been accused of several things, including lying to parliament, and this has delighted the members of the Opposition party;* ***all is grist that comes to their mill****.* ♦ *There have been complaints that the shop-owner is selling alcohol to young people who are under age, but he never asks for proof of age. As far as he is concerned,* ***all is grist that comes to his mill****.*

Help

The proverb is commonly found in the form **all grist to the (someone's) mill**:

♦ *The head teacher is trying to get rid of the art teacher and so any complaints from parents about her are* ***all grist to his mill****.*

'Grist' is a name given to corn that is to be ground into flour.

All roads lead to Rome

There are several different ways or methods of getting the same result: ♦ *There are several different methods of teaching children to read, and I don't think it matters which system you use as long as it's suitable for the child;* ***all roads lead to Rome****.* ♦ *Johnny and Mark both have the same qualifications, although Mark did a full-time university degree course straight from school and Johnny went to evening classes while he was working as a salesman;* ***all roads lead to Rome****.* ♦ *Liz went to drama college for three years and Meg joined a repertory company when she left school. However, both are equally talented and famous actors now and appearing in the same musical production;* ***all roads lead to Rome****.*

Similar

There are more ways of killing a cat than choking it with cream.

Did you know?

It has been suggested that the origin of the proverb lies in the fact that, during the Roman Empire, the Romans built a system of roads, and any of these roads would take a traveller to Rome if he kept going long enough. However, the proverb may just be a reference to the historical, cultural and spiritual influence of Rome.

All that glitters is not gold

This proverb is used as a warning against judging by appearances, in case you are misled into thinking that someone or something is better than they actually are: ♦ *Jenny thought that her new job with a*

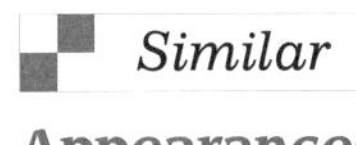

Similar

Appearances are deceptive.

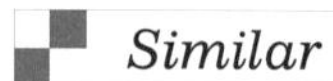

You cannot tell a book by its cover.

*PR company was going to be very glamorous, but she soon learned that **all that glitters is not gold** when she spent all day making coffee and making photocopies of things.* ♦ *The cottage that Harry and Lucy are thinking of buying as a holiday home looks very charming, but they should be aware that **all that glitters is not gold**. The present owners have done a number of things to improve its appearance, but there is a huge amount of work, such as the replacement of the roof, requiring to be done.* ♦ *Beth is completely infatuated by her new next-door neighbour, who is very handsome and well dressed. But Jack knows the man's ex-wife and says that he is a complete rogue; we really ought to warn Beth that **all that glitters is not gold**.*

Did you know?

In origin, the proverb may refer to a line from Shakespeare's *Merchant of Venice*: 'All that glisters is not gold, Often have you heard that told', although the idea is older than that and the verb in Shakespeare's play is 'glisters' and not 'glitters'.

All work and no play makes Jack a dull boy

Everyone needs some leisure and recreation, as working all the time will make them boring and uninteresting: ♦ *It's true that **all work and no play makes Jack a dull boy**; I sat next to Len at dinner last night and all he could talk about was work because he does nothing else.* ♦ *Lucy is a very interesting and entertaining person but her husband, John, spends all his time working and making money; it's a case of **all work and no play makes Jack a dull boy** and John is certainly one of the most boring men I know.* ♦ *You've been studying all day and it will do you good to take a break and go to the cinema; **all work and no play makes Jack a dull boy**.*

Help

The proverb is sometimes found in the humorous feminine form of **all work and no play makes Jill a dull girl**. The name 'Jack' is often found in English to mean every man or everyone, as in 'every man jack of them', meaning every one of them.

All's fair in love and war

Any course of action to achieve victory in love or war can be regarded as acceptable. The expression is also extended to other situations where strong emotion or a strong sense of rivalry or competitiveness is involved: ♦ *When Jim discovered that John was planning to ask Lucy out, he asked her out first;* ***all's fair in love and war****, I suppose.* ♦ *Peter knew that Jack was on the point of asking Jane to marry him when he asked her out; still, Jane shouldn't have agreed to go if she was all that fond of Jack even though* ***all's fair in love and war****.* ♦ *Helen saw the advertisement for the job on the university noticeboard first, removed the notice, applied for the job and got it in the absence of other applicants. It was not an honourable thing to do but she claims that* ***all's fair in love and war****.*

All's well that ends well

If a situation has a satisfactory or happy ending, it does not matter what difficulties or problems occurred before that: ♦ *When Lucy first arrived here, she was very homesick for her own country, but now she loves her life here;* ***all's well that ends well****.* ♦ *We've had a really horrible journey, but we're safely home now;* ***all's well that ends well****.* ♦ ***All's well that ends well****; the parcel was delayed in the post, and we thought it had gone missing, but it has just arrived.*

Help

This is the title of a play by Shakespeare, but the play is not the origin of the saying. It was in common use long before the play and in modern times has become a cliché.

An apple a day keeps the doctor away

Eating an apple every day will keep someone healthy and free from illness: ♦ *I wish the children would eat more fruit; I've tried telling them that* ***an apple a day keeps the doctor away****, but they don't pay any attention.* ♦ *You should eat an apple as a snack between meals instead of chocolate;* ***an apple a day keeps the doctor away****, so they say, and too much chocolate is bad for you.* ♦ *I always take an apple for lunch as well as sandwiches;* ***an apple a day keeps the doctor away****, as they say.*

Did you know?

As is the case with many old sayings, there is some truth in this, as apples, like most other fruits, can contribute to good health. They are thought to be beneficial in dealing with digestive problems and it is highly possible that the play proverb was a polite way of saying that an apple a day kept the bowels regular and prevented constipation.

An old poacher makes the best gamekeeper

Similar

Set a thief to catch a thief.

Someone who has some experience of wrongdoing is the best person to catch people who are doing wrong: ♦ *Harry is a reformed criminal, but he still has a lot of criminal connections and the police use him as an informer;* ***an old poacher makes the best gamekeeper****.* ♦ *The young teacher had frequently played truant himself when he was at school. He knew the places in the town where truants were most likely to be found;* ***an old poacher makes the best gamekeeper****.* ♦ *Meg was a recovering drug addict herself and was able to tell the* *police where the major drug dealers operated in the town;* ***an old poacher makes the best gamekeeper****.*

Any port in a storm

When you are in great difficulty or danger any available help or solution is welcome, whether you like the source of the help or not: ♦ *The town was packed with visitors and the only hotel we could find was very small and uncomfortable; it was very much a case of* ***any port in a storm****.* ♦ *I don't really like asking my neighbour to babysit because she is very busy with her own children. But our usual babysitter was taken ill suddenly and it was* ***any port in a storm****, as they say.* ♦ *There were only two restaurants in the small town and neither of them looked very good, but we were all extremely hungry by then and we said, '****Any port in a storm****.'*

Similar

Beggars can't be choosers.

Needs must when the Devil drives.

Did you know?

This proverb is nautical in origin. It refers to the fact that, particularly in the days of sailing ships, if a ship was caught in a storm at sea, it would make for the nearest port, whether or not it was a port which it usually stopped at.

Appearances are deceptive

You cannot judge someone's character or predict their likely behaviour from how they look. The proverb is often used as a warning to wait and see what a person is really like: ♦ *She looked like a prim, law-abiding old lady, but in fact she was a notorious thief;* ***appearances are deceptive****.* ♦ *The Jackson twins looked very neat and angelic, but the new teacher soon discovered that* ***appearances are deceptive****.* ♦ *The new teacher looks very stern and unapproachable, but she is actually very kind and understanding;* ***appearances are deceptive****.*

Similar

All that glitters is not gold.

You cannot tell a book by its cover.

As you make your bed, so you must lie on it

Similar

As you sow, so you reap.

Sow the wind and reap the whirlwind.

You must accept the consequences of your actions, however unpleasant these may be: ♦ *Ron insisted on marrying Jane in the middle of his medical studies and now he is finding it almost impossible to study and work as a barman in the evenings to support his wife and child; still,* ***as you make your bed, so you must lie on it****.* ♦ *Sara is finding it very difficult getting another well-paid job after she flew into a temper and resigned from her post as head of human resources in Wilson's, but* ***as you make your bed, so you must lie on it****.* ♦ ***As you make your bed, so you must lie on it****; Bill refused to have anything to do with his son after he married Mary against his wishes. Now he is a lonely old man and never sees his grandchildren.*

Help

The proverb is sometimes used in sentences such as **you have made your bed and must lie on it**:

♦ *Jack's* ***made his bed and he must lie on it****; his wife would not have left him if he had agreed to stop gambling.*

Such sentences are sometimes shortened to **you have made your bed**:

♦ *Anne regrets breaking off her engagement, but Tom has another girlfriend now; she's* ***made her bed****.*

As you sow, so you reap

Similar

As you make your bed, so you must lie on it.

Sow the wind and reap the whirlwind.

You will eventually have to accept the consequences of your actions: ♦ *Harry treated his parents very badly and so no one was sorry when Harry's son refused to have anything to do with him;* ***as you sow, so you reap****.* ♦ *Anna has been extravagant all her life, never bothering to save. Now that she is old, she has barely enough to live on;* ***as you sow, so you reap****.* ♦ *Tom is quite bright, but he refused to put any effort into his studies when he was at school and now he has too few qualifications to get a good job;* ***as you sow, so you reap****.*

Help

A slightly more formal version of the proverb is **as you sow, so shall you reap**, while a more modern version is **you reap what you sow**:

♦ *Jenny has spent all term going out to parties and now she is having to stay up all night to study for the exams:* ***you reap what you sow****.* ♦ ***You reap what you sow****; Jessie was her office's greatest gossip, but now that her affair with her boss is known, she is the talk of the office.*

Did you know?

The proverb has a biblical origin, being a reference to Galatians 6:7. It is based on the idea of sowing seeds and gathering the crops which the seeds grow into.

Ask a silly question and you get a silly answer

If you ask someone a foolish or unnecessary question, you cannot expect to get a serious, helpful answer: ♦ *There was an enormous amount of work to be done on the house and when I asked Fred how long he thought it would take to finish it, he said, 'How long is a piece of string?';* ***ask a silly question and you get a silly answer****.* ♦ *Jane was nervous and kept asking Tom the time until he got annoyed and answered, 'Five minutes later than it was the last time you asked me';* ***ask a silly question and you get a silly answer****.*

Help

The proverb is often used in the shortened form **ask a silly question**:

♦ *When I asked Mary when she thought she would have enough money to put down a deposit on a flat, she said, 'The twelfth of never';* ***ask a silly question****.* ♦ *A colleague asked an exhausted-looking Jack what life as a single parent with four kids was like. He replied, 'All fun and games'—* ***ask a silly question****.*

Ask no questions and hear no lies

Curiosity killed the cat.

The proverb is used to discourage an inquisitive person from asking questions: *The children have been asking questions all morning and giving me a headache. I tried saying '**Ask no questions and hear no lies**', but it didn't make any difference.* ♦ *Margaret's young pupils kept asking her how old she was, but she just replied, '**Ask no questions and hear no lies**.'* ♦ *You should really stop trying to get information out of Grace about her private life because she won't tell you anything important anyhow; **ask no questions and you'll hear no lies**.*

Help

An alternative common form of the proverb is **ask no questions and you'll be told no lies**.

Attack is the best form of defence

When you are under attack or in trouble of some kind and likely to be blamed or criticized, it is better to tackle the situation in a positive, aggressive way than be submissive. This proverb now usually refers to verbal attack, although originally it referred to physical attack: ♦ *If you've heard that your boss has been complaining about your work, but hasn't said anything to you, you should go and ask to discuss it with him; **attack is the best form of defence**.* ♦ *The politician knew that he was going to be accused of lack of action by the Opposition party, and so made a speech about how little they had done when they were in government on the grounds that **attack is the best form of defence**.* ♦ ***Attack is the best form of defence**; if Amy is telling people that you have been lying, you should confront her and ask her for proof.*

B

Bad news travels fast

News about something unfortunate or unpleasant gets communicated from person to person very rapidly: ♦ *By the time Jack reached home that evening, the whole street knew that he had lost his job;* ***bad news travels fast****.* ♦ *Sally's parents heard that she had failed her exam before she had an opportunity to tell them herself;* ***bad news travels fast****.* ♦ *Pam realized that all her friends knew that her son had been arrested by the police;* ***bad news travels fast****.*

Similar

No news is good news.

Help

The suggestion behind this proverb is that many people like to gossip and bad news is more likely to be passed on quickly, since it makes more interesting gossip than good news.

Beauty is in the eye of the beholder

The appreciation and assessment of beauty depend on the taste and attitude of the person looking at it and, therefore, are subjective rather than objective: ♦ *Joe told us that his new girlfriend was very beautiful, but she seemed very ordinary to us when we met her; I suppose* ***beauty is in the eye of the beholder****.* ♦ *Bert paid a lot of money to an interior decorator to redecorate and refurnish his house, but I think it's hideous; still,* ***beauty is in the eye of the beholder****.* ♦ *Jane thinks her dog is very attractive, but Jim says it's an ugly little thing;* ***beauty is in the eye of the beholder****, as they say.*

Beauty is only skin deep

Physical beauty is only the most obvious form of attractiveness and is no guarantee that the person who has it will have an attractive temperament, good character, etc: ♦ *Sally is very beautiful, but* ***beauty is only skin deep*** *and she's not at all a likeable person.* ♦ *Peter should learn that* ***beauty is only skin deep****; he always judges women by what they look like.* ♦ *Mark has asked Jill to go out with him and he's very handsome, but she says that* ***beauty is only skin deep*** *and that she prefers men with a bit more personality.*

Beggars can't be choosers

Similar

Any port in a storm.

Needs must when the Devil drives.

Someone who is in great need of something is not in a position to be selective and must take what they are offered, although they might well not have taken it from choice: ♦ *The flat which Jim was offered was tiny and very dark, but it was the only one available which he could afford and* ***beggars can't be choosers****.* ♦ *Pam didn't really like the raincoat but it was the only one in her size in the shop, and the rain was pouring down; she had to accept the fact that* ***beggars can't be choosers****.* ♦ *Sara doesn't like driving large cars, but that one is the only one the hire company has left this weekend and she needs to hire a car urgently to go and visit her mother;* ***beggars can't be choosers****, as they say.*

Believe nothing of what you hear and only half of what you see

Do not be so gullible as to believe all the news, rumours and gossip which you might hear and do not place complete trust in what you see: ♦ *Joan is so naïve that she believes everything she hears and reads. Someone should tell her to say to herself, '****Believe nothing of what you hear and only half of what you see****.'* ♦ *Stan certainly believes absolutely in the saying '****Believe nothing of what you hear and only half of what you see****'; he's the most sceptical person I know.* ♦ *The conditions in the country are chaotic now. Take my advice:* ***Believe nothing of what you hear and only half of what you see****.*

Better be safe than sorry

It is better to be careful and to avoid risks than to be careless and have to feel regretful about having been involved in some kind of accident, trouble or danger: ♦ *We're keeping our child away from her friend Amy just now; Amy's got some kind of infectious disease and* ***better be safe than sorry****.* ♦ *We're leaving the central heating on while we're away in case it gets very cold; we don't want to have any burst pipes and* ***better be safe than sorry****.* ♦ ***Better be safe than sorry****; it doesn't look as though it will rain, but I'm taking my umbrella, anyway.*

Similar

It is best to be on the safe side.

Discretion is the better part of valour.

Help

The proverb is also often found in the slightly shorter form of **better safe than sorry**:

♦ *Do drive very slowly on those icy roads, although the journey will take longer;* ***better safe than sorry****.*

In the shorter form it has become a cliché.

Better late than never

It is better to arrive somewhere later than arranged or expected than never to arrive at all, or to do something later than planned than never to do it at all: ♦ *We had problems with the car and arrived at the party much later than the rest of the guests; still,* ***better late than never****, and our host was very gracious about it.* ♦ *The cheque was delayed in the post and has only just arrived; I was beginning to get worried about it, but* ***better late than never****.* ♦ *We thought the builders were not going to turn up, but they finally arrived and started work two hours late; I suppose it was a case of* ***better late than never****.*

Help

The proverb is frequently used by someone as an excuse for their lateness and has become a cliché.

Better the devil you know than the devil you don't know

Opposite

Familiarity breeds contempt.

It is better to deal with someone whom you know and with whom you are familiar, although they may have faults and you may not like them, than to choose to deal with someone about whom you know nothing and who may turn out to be worse than the person whom you do know: ♦ *James can't stand his boss and is talking of trying to get a job with one of his firm's competitors, but it might well be a case of* ***better the devil you know than the devil you don't know****.* ♦ *Jenny is thinking changing her driving instructor, but she really doesn't enjoy driving and is very nervous. It may not be the instructor's fault that she's not doing well and we are all reminding her of the saying '****Better the devil you know than the devil you don't know****'.*

Help

The proverb can also be used to apply to a place or object as well as a person:

♦ *I thought of replacing my computer, which is not very reliable, but I could only afford a cheap, second-hand one and you know what they say, '****Better the devil you know than the devil you don't know****.'*

It is a very well-known proverb and is often shortened to the form **better the devil you know**:

♦ *We've decided to go back to the place where we've been on holiday the last few years; we've heard so many holiday horror stories from our friends that we've decided that it's a case of* ***better the devil you know****.*

Birds of a feather flock together

Similar

Like will to like.

A man is known by the company he keeps.

People who have similar interests or attitudes like to be together: ♦ *I should warn you that the troublemakers in the class always go around in a group;* ***birds of a feather flock together****, as you know.* ♦ *There's a gang of youths who hang around the shopping mall all day and they've all been in trouble with the police;* ***birds of a feather flock together*** *and so it's no wonder that they're always together.*

Help

The proverb is usually used to refer to people of whom the speaker disapproves. It is a very common proverb and is often shortened to **birds of a feather**, which has become a cliché:

♦ *My neighbour's daughter used to be a quiet, polite girl, but she's turned into a noisy, extremely rude teenager and the friends who visit her are just the same;* ***birds of a feather****, as they say.*

The phrase is often used as an idiom in a sentence:

♦ *People assume that Jim and Joe are* ***birds of a feather****, just because they're friends, but Joe is a very studious boy and Jim never spends any time studying.*

Blood is thicker than water

The relationship between members of the same family is stronger and more important than other relationships: ♦ *Sally and her sister Grace had had a quarrel several years ago and did not speak to each other, but Sally was the first to defend Grace when people started criticizing her; it must be true that* ***blood is thicker than water****.* ♦ *Mary was shocked when her husband took his brother's side and not hers when the two were arguing, but Mary's mother said, '****Blood's thicker than water****.'* ♦ *I know that Bert is one of your best friends, but you can't be sure that he will vote for you in the election; his cousin Will is also one of the candidates for club president and* ***blood's thicker than water****.*

Blood will tell

Inherited characteristics or family traits cannot be concealed and can become obvious: ♦ *It's hardly surprising that Bob has started breaking the law because his father and two of his uncles have been in prison several times;* ***blood will tell****.* ♦ *Meg is the brightest student in the class, which is to be expected as both of her parents are university lecturers;* ***blood will tell****.* ♦ *No wonder Helen has turned out to be so slovenly and idle; her mother and grandmother were just the same and* ***blood will tell****.*

What's bred in the bone will come out in the flesh.

The apple never falls far from the tree.

Boys will be boys

It is a natural part of the growing-up process for boys to be mischievous or unruly. The proverb is often used indulgently to excuse bad behaviour in boys: ♦ *I complained to my next-door neighbour about her sons stealing apples from my tree, but she just smiled and said, '**Boys will be boys**.'* ♦ *The police say that too many parents are taking the attitude that **boys will be boys** and not bothering to discipline their sons.* ♦ *When my friend visited me with her young son, he started pulling the heads of the flowers in the garden and she just looked at him fondly, saying, '**Boys will be boys**.'*

C

Charity begins at home

You should make sure that you look after yourself and your family before considering the welfare of others: ♦ *The local doctor always takes great care of his patients, but his own children are rather neglected; someone should point out to him that **charity begins at home**.* ♦ *Pam's mother is always knitting garments for other people but never anything for her own family and Pam has just reminded her that **charity begins at home**.* ♦ *People regard Jack as a very generous man, because he always gives money to good causes, but his wife and children are often hungry and in need of new clothes; it is time that he remembered that **charity begins at home**.*

Cheats never prosper

People who cheat never do well. This proverb is often directed at people suspected of cheating at cards or other games: ♦ *'**Cheats never prosper**!' said the boy to his opponent at chess whom he thought had cheated, but his opponent denied this vehemently.* ♦ *Sam complained to his mother that many of his classmates* *had got higher marks than him in the test only because they had cheated. It wasn't much consolation, however, when his mother said, 'Don't worry,* ***cheats never prosper****.'* ♦ *The boy who scored the winning goal in the final of the local schools' football competition was accused by the losing side of committing a foul which had gone unnoticed by the referee. He was therefore hounded by shouts of '****Cheats never prosper****!' as he left the stadium to go home.*

Children should be seen and not heard

Children should not draw attention to themselves by being noisy or talkative and so make a nuisance of themselves to adults. This proverb expreses an old-fashioned sentiment: ♦ *In Victorian England the majority of people thought that* ***children should be seen and not heard****.* ♦ *Nowadays it is thought important that children be allowed to play freely and to express themselves, even in the company of adults; the idea that* ***children should be seen and not heard*** *is considered very old-fashioned.*

Did you know?

Originally, the proverb applied only to girls or young women, as in **a maid should be seen and not heard**, 'maid' here meaning girl or young unmarried woman. It was thought important that girls were modest and shy.

Cleanliness is next to godliness

Being clean is second in importance only to being religious and pious: ♦ *Rob belongs to some weird religious sect, but it is obviously not one which believes that* ***cleanliness is next to godliness*** *because he looks as though he has not washed himself, or his clothes, for months.* ♦ *My grandmother brought all her children up to believe that* ***cleanliness is next to godliness*** *and her house was always spotless.*

Clothes make the man

Similar

Fine feathers make fine birds.

Smart, elegant clothes can improve the appearance greatly and people tend to judge other people by how they look: ♦ *You should wear your best suit if you are going for a job interview;* ***clothes make the man****.* ♦ *Sally spends a huge proportion of her salary on clothes, but she says that she has no choice because people are expected to look ultra-smart if they work in PR; it's one of those jobs where it's a case of* ***clothes make the man****.* ♦ *Jim has just been promoted from the factory floor to management and is going to have to wear smart clothes instead of his overalls. He doesn't want to spend a lot of money on them but his wife says that, in office jobs,* ***clothes make the man*** *and Jim is very ambitious.*

Help

An older form of this proverb is **clothes maketh the man** and an alternative, less common, form is **apparel makes the man**.

Confession is good for the soul

Similar

Honesty is the best policy.

Admitting that you have done wrong makes you a better person and can make you feel better: ♦ *I felt really bad about not telling the truth to Jane and decided to admit that I had been lying;* ***confession is good for the soul****.* ♦ *Sara's parents didn't actually realize that she had gone to the nightclub against their wishes, but she was feeling bad about deceiving them and decided to tell them;* ***confession is good for the soul****.* ♦ *Ruth had a guilty conscience about borrowing her sister's dress without her permission or knowledge and she eventually apologized to her sister;* ***confession is good for the soul****.*

Did you know?

The original version of the proverb was **open confession is good for the soul**. In some religions, such as Roman Catholicism, people regularly get priests to hear their confessions of wrongdoing so that they may receive absolution.

Curiosity killed the cat

Showing too much interest in someone else's affairs can be harmful or damaging to you. This proverb is used to discourage someone from asking questions and seeking information: ♦ ***Curiosity killed the cat****; Harry will get really angry if you go on asking him questions about his private affairs.* ♦ *The children tried very hard to find out where their Christmas presents were hidden, but all their mother would say was, '****Curiosity killed the cat****.'* ♦ *When Tom hurt his leg climbing into the old cottage to see what was stored there, his father said, '****Curiosity killed the cat****; you were told to stay away from there.'*

Ask no questions and hear no lies.

Cut your coat according to your cloth

You must take your resources into account when you are planning your actions and not assume that you have more resources than you actually have; this is usually a warning to live within your income: ♦ ***Cut your coat according to your cloth****; your father can't possibly afford the elaborate wedding which you have planned.* ♦ *You may well be able to afford a flat like that in a few years' time, but, at the moment, you can only afford something much smaller;* ***cut your coat according to your cloth****.* ♦ *The holiday which you suggest is far too expensive and you should think of something much nearer home and much cheaper;* ***cut your coat according to your cloth****.*

Help

The proverb is also commonly used as a verbal phrase:

♦ *Joe certainly doesn't believe in* ***cutting his coat according to his cloth****; he's already in debt and he's just taken out a huge loan to pay for that car.* ♦ *The rent on my flat has been increased by a lot and I won't have much money to spend on going out; I'll just have to* ***cut my coat according to my cloth****.*

D

Dead men tell no tales

People cannot make any comments or give any information when they are dead: ♦ *The gunman killed himself after he had killed the two youths and it is unlikely that we will ever find out what happened;* ***dead men tell no tales****.* ♦ *The fort had obviously been attacked and all the people within it killed, but there was no indication as to who had carried out the killings;* ***dead men tell no tales****.* ♦ *What exactly happened in the village will probably never be known; all the villagers were massacred and* ***dead men tell no tales****.*

Death is the great leveller

Death makes everyone equal, whatever inequalities there have been in life, since wealth, and the power and privilege which it brings with it, cannot be taken beyond the grave: ♦ ***Death is the great leveller*** *since corpses cannot take their money with them.* ♦ *Harry was a very wealthy, arrogant man with a great deal of power and his brother was penniless. However, as I looked at their two graves, I could not help thinking how irrelevant all that was now:* ***death is the great leveller****.* ♦ *The owner of the factory and one of the cleaners both died in the fire and were buried on the same day in the same graveyard;* ***death is the great leveller****.*

Similar

Never put off till tomorrow what you can do today.

Procrastination is the thief of time.

Tomorrow never comes.

Delays are dangerous

This proverb warns against putting things off instead of doing them right away: ♦ *The government should finalize the details of its traffic policy;* ***delays are dangerous****.* ♦ *The president was right to send in troops right away;* ***delays are dangerous****.* ♦ *The building contractor now has permission to start building the block of flats and he should get on with it right away;* ***delays are dangerous****.*

Desperate diseases must have desperate remedies

Urgent or serious situations require to be dealt with by urgent or serious action: ♦ *Tom had to sell his house to pay his son's legal bills when he was charged with murder;* ***desperate diseases must have desperate remedies.*** ♦ *Although Pam was highly qualified, the only job which she could get was that of office cleaner, but she had three children to feed and* ***desperate diseases must have desperate remedies.*** ♦ *Jill attends college lectures during the day and she should really spend her evenings studying. However, she needs to earn money to pay her living expenses and so works as a waitress in a late-night café;* ***desperate diseases must have desperate remedies.***

Help

There are several versions of this proverb, including **desperate diseases must have desperate cures**; **desperate ills must have desperate remedies**; **desperate cuts must have desperate cures**.

Devil take the hindmost

See **Every man for himself**.

Diamond cuts diamond

This proverb is used of a situation in which two people who are in competition with each other are equally clever or cunning: ♦ *The talks relating to the takeover bid are likely to go on for some time. The chief executive of the company which has put in the bid is a very clever and experienced negotiator, but so is the chief executive of the company which is being taken over; and so it is a case of* ***diamond cuts diamond.*** ♦ *Sometimes there is one student in a class who is much cleverer than the rest, but in this particular class there are two students who are very evenly matched in ability and either of them could win the medal for best student;* ***diamond cuts***

***diamond**. ♦ Tim is very clever and well informed, but he tended to go out with girls who were not all that clever until he met Mary, who is just as clever as he is; at last, **diamond cuts diamond**.*

Discretion is the better part of valour

Similar

Better be safe than sorry.

He who fights and runs away, may live to fight another day.

It is best to be cautious and not to take unnecessary risks, although such caution may appear to be rather cowardly: ♦ *Some of the MPs must have privately disagreed with the prime minister's statement. However, being ambitious, they decided to keep silent rather than risk his anger; it was one of those times when **discretion is the better part of valour**.* ♦ *Sara always said exactly what she thought, refusing to believe that **discretion is the better part of valour**, and consequently was not at all popular with her employers.*

Distance lends enchantment to the view

Similar

Absence makes the heart grow fonder.

Opposite

Out of sight, out of mind.

Things or people which appear attractive or desirable when they are at a distance, or not present, may not appear so when they are close at hand: ♦ *Joe used to visit the city once a year and thought that it would be wonderful to live and work there. Alas, when he eventually got a job in the city, he hated the noise and the crowds and soon went back home; **distance lends enchantment to the view**.* ♦ *Sally envied her friends who shared a flat rather than living with their parents. However, when she went to live with them for a week, she realized that she much preferred the comforts of home; as her mother said, '**Distance lends enchantment to the view**.'* ♦ *Jenny and Meg had just become good friends when Meg's family moved to the other end of the country and they missed each other very much, telephoning regularly and exchanging frequent letters. Sadly, it was a case of **distance lends enchantment to the view**, because* *when Meg's family moved back, the two girls discovered that they had nothing much in common and did not really like each other.*

Help

The proverb often appears in the shortened form **distance lends enchantment**:

♦ *Tom heard tales from his grandparents about how wonderful life was in the country where they had been born. But **distance lends enchantment**; when Tom went there on a visit, he found that it was a poverty-stricken place where the people were very unhappy.*

Divide and rule

This proverb indicates that, in order to achieve and maintain a position of complete control and authority, it is important to make sure that the people under your control quarrel among themselves, thus making it less likely that they will unite to overthrow you: ♦ *None of the club members really like the president, but it is a case of **divide and rule**; they all argued among themselves about choosing a replacement. In the end, they couldn't agree and the president was re-elected.* ♦ *The workers in the factory did not all belong to the same trade union and the managers were trying to adopt a policy of **divide and rule** by making separate agreements with each of the unions, some less favourable than others.* ♦ *The king was afraid that some of the nobles might plot to overthrow him, and perhaps kill him, and so he did his best to cause trouble and rivalry among them; it was much safer for him to pursue a policy of **divide and rule**.*

Do as I say, not as I do

This proverb is used to indicate to someone that they should act or behave as instructed by the user of the proverb and should not copy the actions or behaviour of the user; sometimes used humorously:

Opposite

Example is better than precept.

♦ *My father made me promise never to smoke, although he himself smokes. When I pointed this out, he simply said, '**Do as I say, not as I do**.'* ♦ *The teacher told the class to answer all the questions in sentences, although she herself was just going to write 'yes' or 'no', saying '**Do as I say, not as I do**.'* ♦ *My brother kept saying '**Do as I say, not as I do**' when he was teaching his wife to drive and completely confused her.*

Do as you would be done by

Treat other people in the manner in which you would like them to treat you: ♦ *'You can't expect your neighbours to be kind to your children when you are always shouting at theirs. **Do as you would be done by**,' said Lucy to Sally.* ♦ *Ken frequently borrows books from John, but he has just refused to lend John one of his reference books and I felt that I had to say to him, '**Do as you would be done by**.'* ♦ *A great many people do not seem to believe in the proverb **Do as you would be done by**, expecting other people to treat them with kindness and politeness, while they themselves treat others rudely.*

Did you know?

Another more formal version of this proverb is **do unto others as you would they should do unto you**, a biblical allusion to Luke 6:31—'As ye would that men should do to you, do ye also to them likewise.'

Don't change horses in mid-stream

This proverb advises against making changes after you have already started a project, particularly a change which involves stopping supporting one person, belief, etc, and starting to support another: ♦ *You've supported that political party all your life and there's no reason to change your mind in the middle of an election campaign; **don't change horses in mid-stream**.* ♦ *Judy is talking about changing from a science degree course to an arts one,* *but her director of studies has told her* ***not to change horses in mid-stream*** *without giving the matter a great deal of consideration.*

Help

The proverb is sometimes found in the form **don't swap horses in mid-stream**, and phrases formed from both are often used alone:

♦ *Molly was studying medicine, but she found the course too long and too difficult and decided to* ***change horses in mid-stream*** *and study for a degree in biology.* ♦ *At the start of the election campaign for students' representative, Mike said that he was going to support Lucy, but he* ***swapped horses in mid-stream*** *and voted for Linda.*

Did you know?

In origin, the proverb refers to the difficulty, and possible danger, encountered by a rider who tries to dismount from one horse and mount another while fording a river.

Don't count your chickens before they are hatched

This proverb advises people not to be sure that something for which they are hoping will actually happen because the outcome might be quite different and they will be disappointed: ♦ ***don't count your chickens before they are hatched****; several other people are interested in buying the house you want and they may offer the seller more money than you can afford.* ♦ *You may not have won the election because there are still quite a lot of votes to be counted;* ***don't count your chickens before they are hatched****.*

Similar

First catch your hare.

There's many a slip 'twixt cup and lip.

Help

The proverb is often found in the shortened form **don't count your chickens**, which has become a cliché:

♦ *You got the right answer, but a lot of people entered the competition and you might not have won;* ***don't count your chickens****.*

The phrase **count your chickens** is also commonly used:

♦ *Jim had already decided how he was going to spend the prize money, but he* **shouldn't have counted his chickens** *because he didn't win the competition after all.* ♦ *Beth was so sure that she had got the job as supervisor that she resigned from her existing job and then she heard that somebody with more experience had got the supervisor's job; what a pity that she* **counted her chickens**.

Don't cross the bridge till you come to it

Similar

Don't cry before you are hurt.

Don't meet trouble halfway.

Never trouble trouble until trouble troubles you.

You should not worry about something before it actually happens; it may never happen and you will have caused yourself unnecessary anxiety: ♦ ***Don't cross the bridge till you come to it****; just because you've heard that some workers might lose their jobs, it doesn't necessarily mean that you will lose yours.* ♦ *The rumour that your landlord is thinking of selling your flat is not necessarily true;* **don't cross the bridge till you come to it**. ♦ *You shouldn't worry about failing the exam until you get the results because you might have done better than you think;* **don't cross the bridge till you come to it**.

Help

Part of the proverb is commonly found as an idiom in sentences:

♦ *Jenny is always* **crossing bridges before she comes to them**; *she is worrying that her mother might not be able to look after the children next week when she hasn't even asked her yet.* ♦ *If we discover that the house we like is in need of a lot of expensive repairs, we'll* **cross that bridge when we come to it**; *there's no point in worrying now.*

Don't cry before you are hurt

Similar

Don't cross the bridge till you come to it.

Don't meet trouble halfway.

You should not complain or worry about something before it actually happens; it may never happen and you will have been complaining or worrying unnecessarily: ♦ *I know your parents have threatened to reduce your allowance, but they were angry and they might not actually do it;* ***don't cry before you are hurt***. ♦ *You don't know for certain that* *your landlord is going to increase the rent;* ***don't cry before you are hurt****.* ♦ *The repairs to your car might not be nearly as expensive as you think they're going to be;* ***don't cry before you are hurt****.*

Don't cut off your nose to spite your face

This proverb is used to warn someone not to try to hurt or injure someone else in such a way that it harms themselves: ♦ ***Don't cut off your nose to spite your face****; if you punish the children by not letting them play outside on such a beautiful day, you'll have to stay inside with them and deprive yourself of the sunshine.* ♦ ***Don't cut your nose off to spite your face****; if you refuse to take the children on holiday because they've been naughty, you won't get a holiday either.*

Help

The phrase **cut off your nose to spite your face** is also commonly used, and this is sometimes shortened to **cut off your nose**:

♦ *It became clear that Jane was* ***cutting off her nose*** *by refusing her customers' requests to open her shop on Saturday mornings; most of them took their custom elsewhere, not just on Saturday but the rest of the week as well.*

Don't make a mountain out of a molehill

Don't exaggerate the scale of a problem and make it seem more difficult than it actually is: ♦ *I know that you have to prepare for the party, but* ***don't make a mountain out of a molehill****; there are only six people coming.* ♦ *Admittedly, it's a long journey to the town where Jane lives, but there is a direct train from here to there;* ***don't make a mountain out of a molehill****.* ♦ *It's unfortunate that the football coach has resigned, but* ***don't make a mountain out of a molehill****; there* *are a lot of qualified people around and we have plenty of time to appoint someone before the new season starts.*

Help

The phrase **make a mountain out of a molehill** is also commonly used and has become a cliché:

♦ *Jane is hysterical about the fact that we are going to have to find a new venue for the party, but she is always **making mountains out of molehills**.* ♦ *Bob said that his car was in a very bad condition when Bill returned it to him, but there was scarcely a scratch on it; Bob was just **making a mountain out of a molehill**.*

Don't meet trouble halfway

There is no point in worrying about something before it actually happens; do not anticipate trouble: ♦ *They say that your car is very likely to be repaired before you go on holiday; **don't meet trouble halfway**.* ♦ *Just because Jack has been declared redundant doesn't mean that you will be; **don't meet trouble halfway**.* ♦ *There is probably a simple explanation for Jim being late; **don't meet trouble halfway** by assuming that he's been in an accident.*

Similar

Don't cross the bridge till you come to it.

Don't cry before you are hurt.

Never trouble trouble until trouble troubles you.

Don't put all your eggs in one basket

Don't put all your resources into one venture or course of action, since you will lose everything if the venture or course of action is unsuccessful: ♦ *Ken says that he is going to invest all his savings in his brother's new business, although friends have advised him, '**Don't put all your eggs in one basket**.'* ♦ ***Don't put all your eggs in one basket**; you should send in job applications to several firms, not just apply to the company which you prefer. There are very few jobs in publishing and a great many people are looking for them.* ♦ ***Don't put all your eggs in one basket**; you should do what all the other students are doing and apply to several universities, in case you are not accepted for the course of your choice.*

Help

The phrase **put all your eggs in one basket** is also commonly used and has become a cliché:

♦ *Sadly, Jill has been guilty of* ***putting all her eggs in one basket****; she sold all her assets, including her house and car, and invested the money in her boyfriend's antique shop. It has now gone bust.* ♦ *We tried to warn Tom against* ***putting all his eggs in one basket****, but he was so sure he would get the job he applied for that he didn't apply for any others. Now he is unemployed.*

Don't spoil the ship for a ha'porth of tar

Do not economize on things which do not cost a lot or do not involve much effort, when doing so might put at risk the success of a project: ♦ ***Don't spoil the ship for a ha'porth of tar****; you have spent a great deal of money on rebuilding and renovating the house and it will ruin the effect if you put down such a cheap carpet.* ♦ *You really should try to buy some new shoes to go with your smart new dress and hat;* ***don't spoil the ship for a ha'porth of tar****.* ♦ *You've obviously spent a great deal of time getting the house ready and preparing the food and drink for tonight's party, but it would be nice to have some fresh flowers;* ***don't spoil the ship for a ha'porth of tar****.*

Similar

If a thing's worth doing, it's worth doing well.

Help

The phrase **spoil the ship for a ha'porth of tar** is also commonly used and is sometimes shortened to **spoil the ship**:

♦ *I don't know why Dick decided to build those cheap bookcases in that lovely house; he's certainly* ***spoilt the ship****.*

Did you know?

The proverb does not, as you would suppose, have a nautical origin, but an agricultural one. The word 'sheep' is pronounced 'ship' in some English dialects and tar was applied on sores and wounds on sheep to prevent flies from landing on them and causing further infection. The idea behind the proverb, which originally had the word 'lose' instead of 'spoil', is that the application of a little tar, which would cost very little time or money, would save the sheep's life. In time, the word 'sheep' came to be spelt 'ship' and the proverb was assumed to have a nautical origin, since tar was also used to preserve and repair the surface of ships.

Don't teach your grandmother to suck eggs

Don't try to offer advice or instruction to someone who has more experience and knowledge than you do. The proverb is often used to suppress the advice of young people who are full of new ideas: ♦ ***Don't teach your grandmother to suck eggs****; Pete's been wallpapering rooms since long before you were born.* ♦ *You may have learnt a lot about car maintenance on your college course, but Tony's a qualified mechanic with years of experience;* ***don't teach your grandmother to suck eggs****.* ♦ *You may have learnt a lot about modern marketing methods at college, but Don knows all there is to know about our products and about our customers;* ***don't teach your grandmother to suck eggs****.*

Don't throw the baby out with the bathwater

Be careful that you do not get rid of something good along with the bad things when you are making changes: ♦ *I realize that it's tempting to change the management structure of the firm completely, but the present system does have some good points;* ***don't throw out the baby with the bathwater****.* ♦ ***Don't throw out the baby with the bathwater****; the present system of accounting may be old-fashioned, but some elements of it are very useful.* ♦ *Admittedly, this old house is badly in* *need of modernizing, but some of the original features are very much worth retaining;* ***don't throw out the baby with the bathwater****.*

Help

The phrase **throw out the baby with the bathwater** is also commonly used and has become a cliché:

♦ *There is certainly room for improvement in the marketing department, but the new manager will be* ***throwing out the baby with the bathwater*** *if he sacks all of the advertising staff; there is a great deal of expertise there.*

Don't wash your dirty linen in public

Don't discuss your private affairs in public: ♦ ***Don't wash your dirty linen in public****; you may be upset by the family scandal, but it's not fair to the rest of the family to make it public.* ♦ ***Don't wash your dirty linen in public****; the disagreement over your divorce arrangements concerns no one but yourself and your husband.* ♦ *You're embarrassing the rest of the guests by talking constantly about your money problems;* ***don't wash your dirty linen in public****.*

Help

The phrase **wash your dirty linen in public** is also commonly used and has become a cliché:

♦ *Helen's parents were very annoyed when they heard that she had been* ***washing her dirty linen in public****; they had hope to keep the scandal a secret.*

Did you know?

The proverb is derived from a French proverb which was popularized by Napoleon Bonaparte.

E

Early to bed and early to rise makes a man healthy, wealthy and wise

This proverb recommends going to bed early and getting up early, claiming that this will have important advantages for your physical health, your mental ability and the state of your bank account: ♦ *Ken gets up at about 6 am and is always in bed before 11 pm even now though he has retired from work; '**Early to bed and early to rise makes a man healthy, wealthy and wise**' has long been his motto.* ♦ *'**Early to bed and early to rise makes a man healthy, wealthy and wise**' is not a proverb that is likely to appeal to Tom; he went clubbing last night, came in at 5 am and is still asleep at 4 pm.*

Help

The proverb is very well known, and sometimes only part of it used:

♦ *'**Early to bed and early to rise**' is certainly not the motto of the students who live in the flat above ours; they are usually coming in from a party when we are going to work.* ♦ *I know it's not very late, but I've had a hard day and I have to be at work early tomorrow; it's a case of **early to bed and early to rise**.*

In the shorter form, the proverb has become a cliché.

East, west, home's best

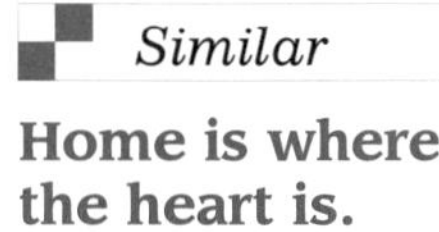

Home is where the heart is.

Travel broadens the mind.

Whatever the attractions and benefits of travel, home is the best place to be: ♦ *Mark plans to work overseas for two years and has been trying to persuade me to go with him, but as far as I'm concerned: **east, west, home's best**.* ♦ *Lucy says that she loved travelling when she was young, but now that she's older, she finds that it's a case of **east, west, home's best**.* ♦ *It is impossible to convince most young people of the truth of the saying '**East, west, home's best**'; they all seem to want to go backpacking round the world as far away from home as possible.*

Easy come, easy go

Money which is acquired with very little effort will be spent just as easily: ♦ *Polly is very extravagant and never asks what something costs before buying; her father gives her a huge allowance and so it's a case of* **easy come, easy go**. ♦ *Jane has had to work all her life just to feed and clothe her family; she really resents her wealthy sister-in-law's attitude of* **easy come, easy go**.

Help

The proverb is sometimes shortened to **easy come**:

♦ *If Fred had to work for a living instead of living on his father's wealth, he wouldn't squander such a lot money; it's a case of* **easy come**.

A less well-known form of the proverb is **lightly come, lightly go**.

Eat to live, not live to eat

This proverb warns that the purpose of food is to keep us alive and that we should eat only enough to do so, instead of being greedy and over-fond of food: ♦ *Jill said that they never went to restaurants when she was a child and never had special family meals because her father's motto was '***Eat to live, not live to eat***.'* ♦ *Bert says that when he was young, his grandmother was always quoting the proverb '***Eat to live, not live to eat***' and that he rebelled against this as he grew older; that is why he's now a restaurant reviewer for a city newspaper.*

Did you know?

The proverb is attributed to Socrates, an ancient Greek philosopher.

Empty vessels make the most sound

People who are the least clever or knowledgeable about something often do the most talking: ♦ *We had hoped that the meeting to protest against the building of the new road would be successful, but some of the least well-informed protesters kept making stupid comments and would not let the engineering and environment experts speak;* ***empty vessels make the most sound****.* ♦ *The new head teacher organized a meeting of staff and students so that people could make proposals as to how to improve the school. Unfortunately, a great many of the students spoiled it by making ridiculous suggestions;* ***empty vessels make the most sound****.*

Help

Other versions of the proverb include **empty vessels make the most noise** and **empty vessels make the greatest sound.** The word 'vessel' in the proverb refers to a receptacle or container, such as one for holding a liquid.

Enough is as good as a feast

 *Opposite*

The more you get, the more you want.

If you have enough of something for your needs, then you should be content with that and not want unnecessarily large amounts: ♦ *The flat is very small but it is big enough for the two of us and* ***enough is as good as a feast****.* ♦ *I really enjoy my new job, and although the salary is not as high as in my previous job, I can live on it;* ***enough is as good as a feast****, as they say.* ♦ *We would have preferred a house with a bigger garden, but there is plenty of room in this garden for the children to play and for us to grow some flowers and vegetables. That is all that matters;* ***enough is as good as a feast****.*

Even a worm will turn

Even the meekest, most humble person will start defending themselves, if they are treated badly enough: ♦ *James had been bullied by Tom for so long that he could take it no more. One day he struck Tom, to everyone's amazement;* ***even a worm will turn****.* ♦ *Jane was a very quiet, timid person and her husband was a control freak who was always criticizing her and ordering her about. One night, however, she lost her temper and* *shouted back at him;* ***even a worm will turn****.* ♦ *The office supervisor clearly didn't like Mary, who was a very timid, unassuming person, and regularly criticized her work in front of everyone. But one day, Mary marched off to the manager and reported the supervisor for bullying and harassment;* ***even a worm will turn****.*

Every cloud has a silver lining

Something good will always comes from an unpleasant or difficult situation; there is usually a good side to any unpleasant or difficult situation: ♦ *The family are all going on holiday for a couple of weeks and I'm going to miss them.* ***Every cloud has a silver lining****, however; I will have more leisure time when they're not around.* ♦ ***Every cloud has a silver lining****. If Pam hadn't lost her job, she wouldn't have met Frank at the job centre; now they're going to be married.* ♦ *If it hadn't rained when I was on holiday, I wouldn't have been going round the shops and so I would never have found this lovely antique table;* ***every cloud has a silver lining****.*

Similar

It's an ill wind that blows nobody any good.

Opposite

No rose without a thorn.

Every dog has his day

Every person, however unimportant or unfortunate, has a period of good fortune or success at some point in his or her life. This proverb is often used to give encouragement to someone who is not being very lucky or successful at present: ♦ *I know that you've not had much success in finding a suitable job, but you might get lucky soon;* ***every dog has his day****, you know.* ♦ *Mike was mostly very unhappy and not very successful at school, but he was very pleased when he unexpectedly won the essay competition in his last year;* ***every dog has his day****, as they say.* ♦ *It took John a long time to be promoted to a management post, but he worked very hard and took several college courses until eventually he was successful; it was a case of* ***every dog has his day****.*

Every little helps

You should not disregard a small contribution to something as being unimportant, as small amounts together make a large amount: ♦ *It is a poor area and we know that people will not be able to give large donations to our charity, but* ***every little helps****.* ♦ *They're collecting for things to sell at the church jumble sale but all I can give them is a few books; still,* ***every little helps****, I suppose.* ♦ *I only had a few coins to give to the beggar, but* ***every little helps****; if everyone gave him a few pence, he would soon have the price of a meal.*

Every man for himself

Everyone is concerned with protecting their own interests and with getting as much as possible for themselves. This proverb is usually used in a situation in which it is advisable for someone to concentrate on his or her own interests or safety even if this is to the disadvantage of others: ♦ *There were far more people trying to buy things than there were goods for sale; it was a case of* ***every man for himself****.* ♦ *It was a fierce battle and there was no time or opportunity to make sure that others were all right; it was* ***every man for himself****.* ♦ *Several members of the department are keen to be promoted and they will all be applying for the job aggressively; it will be a case of* ***every man for himself****.*

Help

The proverb has two longer versions. The less common of these is **every man for himself, and God for us all**, which means that, although we all protect our own, individual interests, God looks after all our interests:

♦ *The boxer was told by his trainer that it was likely to be a fierce fight and that it was a case of* ***every man for himself, and God for us all****.*

The more common of the longer versions is **every man for himself, and the Devil take the hindmost**. This means that every man should look after himself and his own interests, not worrying about the interests of others, and that the person who is least successful and comes last will suffer the worst fate:

♦ *There's only room for five people to sleep in the mountain hut and there are six of you; so* ***every man for himself, and the devil take the hindmost****.* ♦ *There are only a few tickets left for the concert and so you should get down to the box office right away or you will be disappointed;* ***every man for himself, and the devil take the hindmost****.*

A shorter version of this last proverb is **devil take the hindmost**, used to warn someone against being last or least successful because of the difficulty or disadvantage that this will bring:

♦ *There are only six places left on the computer course and you should apply now if you are interested;* ***devil take the hindmost****.*

Every man has his price

Money is an attractive lure and people are persuaded to do things which they would not usually do if they are offered a large sum of money to do so: ♦ *We all thought that the manager was far too loyal an employee of the company to go and work for another firm, but one of our competitors offered him a job with a far higher salary and he accepted;* ***every man has his price****, I suppose.* ♦ *We were all astounded to learn that Alice, who was one of our most trusted employees, had been accepting money from a rival firm to give them advance details of our new designs; sadly,* ***every man has his price****.* ♦ *We thought that our nanny was happy with us and she seemed to love our children, but she has just told us that she is going to work for another family; they are very rich and* ***every man has his price****.*

Similar

A golden key can open any door.

Money talks.

Money is power.

Every man to his taste

People's tastes differ and everyone should be allowed to choose what they like and what they dislike: ♦ *Sam has just redecorated his house in bright shades of orange and green; I find it very garish, but* ***every man to his***

Similar

There is no accounting for tastes.

Similar

One man's meat is another man's poison.

taste. ♦ *Sally is well educated and yet the only things she reads are fashion magazines and paperback romances; well,* ***every man to his taste****.* ♦ *Most of the family are spending the summer holiday in a cottage in the country, but our daughter says that the area is too quiet for her and she has decided to stay in the city;* ***every man to his taste****, I suppose.*

Help

An alternative form of the proverb is **everyone to his taste.**

Every man to his trade

Similar

Let the cobbler stick to his last.

People should concentrate on what they are qualified to do and leave other things to those who are qualified to do them: ♦ *Sam likes to try to carry out repairs to the house himself, but Jenny has had bad experiences of this in the past and always calls in a professional tradesman. She believes in the saying '****Every man to his trade****.'* ♦ ***Every man to his trade****; Ron should have sent for a computer engineer when his machine developed a fault instead of trying to fix it himself and ending up having to buy a new computer.* ♦ *Lucy says that '****Every man to his trade****' is her motto and she hires people to do all her household tasks—from doing the laundry to catering for dinner parties to walking the dog.*

Everything has an end

Similar

All good things must come to an end.

This proverb emphasizes the fact that it is inevitable for things to come to an end. It is sometimes used as encouragement for people who are experiencing a period of difficulty or trouble: ♦ *Our summer holiday was wonderful, but* ***everything has an end*** *and we must go back to work tomorrow.* ♦ *It is hard for students to have to spend all their time studying, but* ***everything has an end****; they will have plenty of free time next month after the exams are over.* ♦ ***Everything has an end****; your financial* *situation is very bad just now, I know, but the children will soon be at school and then you'll be able to get a job.*

Example is better than precept

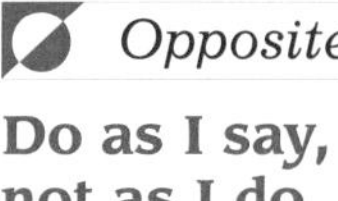

Opposite

Do as I say, not as I do.

It is better to indicate to people what is the right thing to do by your actions, so that they can copy you, rather than by instructions: ♦ *Jane should learn that* ***example is better than precept****; she is always telling her children to be neat and tidy, but she is the untidiest person I know.* ♦ *Bob is always late for his appointments and yet he often lectures the members of his staff on the importance of punctuality; someone should tell him that* ***example is better than precept****.* ♦ *Jill is trying to persuade her children of the importance of eating a balanced, healthy diet but she always eats junk food at lunchtime; it's time she realized that* ***example is better than precept****.*

Experience is the best teacher

This proverb emphasizes the importance of experience in learning something, the implication being that it is more important than qualifications, training or instruction: ♦ *Jim studied engineering at university, but says that he learned far more from working for a few weeks than he had from several years of university study. He's proof of the truth of the old saying '****Experience is the best teacher****.'* ♦ *Sally was thinking of going to drama college but one of her father's friends, who is an actor, has said that, in acting,* ***experience is the best teacher****. She should start auditioning for parts right away or try to join a small repertory company.* ♦ *Bob would like to go to college to do a course in business studies, but his father says that* ***experience is the best teacher*** *and wants Bob to join the family business straight from school.*

F

Fair exchange is no robbery

If one thing is given in exchange for another, particularly when the things are more or less of equal value, then no one has been cheated or robbed: ♦ *Jean and Pat had the same taste in literature and used to buy books and read them before exchanging them with each other; it was a case of* ***fair exchange is no robbery****.* ♦ *Mark had a flat on one side of town and Tom had a very similar flat of roughly the same value on the other side. When they decided to swap, it was a case of* ***fair exchange is no robbery****.* ♦ *Ellen was given some earrings for Christmas which she didn't like and agreed to swap them for a brooch which Joan had been given;* ***fair exchange is no robbery*** *and the donors of the gifts never found out.*

Faith will move mountains

This proverb emphasizes the power which faith, such as religious faith, or a fervent belief in something has: ♦ *The young woman was told by medical experts that she would never be able to have children, but she prayed every day and eventually, to the amazement of the doctors, became pregnant;* ***faith will move mountains****.* ♦ *The old woman was said to be terminally ill with cancer, but she had tremendous faith in the powers of the complementary medicine specialist and she lived for several more years;* ***faith will move mountains****.* ♦ *Bill's parents refused to believe that he was dead, although they were told by army officers that no soldier had survived the battle where he was last seen. However,* ***faith will move mountains****; several years later Bill was released by the enemy forces who had taken him captive during the battle.*

Did you know?

This proverb is biblical in origin, being an allusion to Matthew 17:20—'If ye have faith as a grain of mustard seed, ye shall say unto this mountain "Remove hence to yonder place" and it shall remove.'

Familiarity breeds contempt

If you come to know someone or something very well or become too accustomed to them, you cease to appreciate them and respect them: ♦ *When we first moved near the sea, we used to walk on the beach every day, but now we hardly ever do;* ***familiarity breeds contempt****, I suppose.* ♦ *When Jack first joined the club, he used to have lunch there every day and really enjoyed meeting other club members, but he hasn't been for months now;* ***familiarity breeds contempt****, it seems.* ♦ *Quite a few couples moved into this housing estate at the same time and they all used to meet regularly for a drink and a chat, but that stopped after a year or so. It was probably a case of* ***familiarity breeds contempt****.*

Opposite

Better the devil you know than the devil you don't know.

Fear the Greeks bearing gifts

Beware of someone whom you know to be an enemy or rival when they are making friendly gestures, such as bringing gifts: ♦ *I'm playing John in the tennis tournament final tomorrow morning and tonight he unexpectedly suggested going out for a drink. I suspected that he might be trying to get me drunk and I believe in the old proverb '****Fear the Greeks bearing gifts****.'* ♦ ***Fear the Greeks bearing gifts****; our next-door neighbours, with whom we have had a long feud, have just given us some home-made pots of jam and I wouldn't be surprised if the jam contains something nasty.* ♦ *Sally was advised* ***to fear the Greeks bearing gifts*** *when Jill, who absolutely hates her since she went off with her fiancé, asked her to have lunch with her. Sally heeded* *the warning and declined, worrying that Jill might try to harm her.*

Help

The proverb sometimes takes the form **fear the Greeks even when they are bearing gifts**.

Did you know?

In origin, the proverb is an allusion to the wooden horse which was given by the Greeks to the Trojans, but was actually a means of getting some of their men inside Troy so that they could attack it, since they were hiding inside the horse. According to Virgil's *Aeneid II*, one of the Trojans, Laocoon, is quoted as saying, 'I fear the Greeks, even when bearing gifts' when he was advising against the Trojans letting the wooden horse into their city.

Fine feathers make fine birds

Similar

Clothes make the man.

Smart, elegant clothes can make people look attractive, although they may not be so without them: ♦ *Sally always looks beautiful when you see her at social occasions, but it is because she wears beautifully-cut designer clothes and spends a lot of time at the beauty salon and the hairdresser's. She's actually quite plain and it's very much a case of* ***fine feathers make fine birds****.* ♦ *Paul hired an expensive dinner jacket and looked very handsome at the ball where he met Meg, but she scarcely recognized him next day when he was looking very ordinary in jeans and a sweater;* ***fine feathers make fine birds****, as they say.* ♦ *Mark was amazed when he saw his female office colleagues all dressed up for the office party, looking completely different from their everyday selves. It reminded him that* ***fine feathers make fine birds****.*

Fine words butter no parsnips

Nothing is achieved simply by using fine, elegant words: ♦ *The politician has given several very eloquent speeches about the improvements which the government plans to make to public transport, but nothing ever gets done. We need to remind them that* ***fine words butter no parsnips****.* ♦ *The principal has held several meetings to assure parents that he is drawing up a new strategy for dealing with bullying, but the parents of the children who are being bullied are tired of listening to high-flown jargon and they want action taken against the bullies immediately. They are of the opinion that* ***fine words butter no parsnips****.* ♦ *The education minister has a reputation for being silver-tongued and always gives fluent, lucid statements about the future of education. However, most parents feel that the time for talking is past and that now it's time for constructive action; they have to keep reminding their local MPs that* ***fine words butter no parsnips****.*

Similar

Actions speak louder than words.

Did you know?

In origin, the proverb refers to the fact that parsnips, a root vegetable, are often garnished with butter before serving to improve the flavour.

First catch your hare

There is no point in planning what you are going to do with something until you actually have it: ♦ ***First catch your hare****; there's no point in deciding what you're going to do with your first month's salary when you haven't found a job yet.* ♦ *Beth has decided what furniture she is going to buy for her flat and what colours she is going to use to decorate it, although she hasn't started looking at flats yet and is never going to be able to afford to buy one. I wonder if she's heard of the proverb '****First catch your hare****.'* ♦ *Liz is planning a very elaborate menu, but she won't find many of the ingredients in the local shop and the nearest town is miles away. Those of you who live here should have told her that it's a case of* ***first catch your hare****.*

Similar

Don't count your chickens before they are hatched.

There's many a slip 'twixt cup and lip.

Did you know?

The origin of this proverb is often attributed to Mrs Glasse's *Art of Cookery* (1747), in particular to her recipe for hare soup, but the actual quotation is 'take your hare when it is cased', 'cased' meaning skinned.

First come, first served

Similar

The early bird catches the worm.

This proverb emphasizes the importance of promptness if you wish to obtain or achieve something: ♦ *To promote the new show we are giving away 50 free tickets and it's going to be a case of* ***first come, first served****.* ♦ *I know that you're a regular customer and I'm sorry that you didn't get a free copy of the book, but the publisher only gave us a limited number and we gave them to the first people to arrive at the book-signing;* ***first come, first served****, I'm afraid.* ♦ *We are not accepting advance bookings for the opening night of the new restaurant; it will be* ***first come, first served****.*

First impressions are the most lasting

What you first think of someone or something tends to last a long time and have an effect on your long-term opinion of them: ♦ *Unfortunately, Sally was in an unfriendly, surly mood when she first met Mike's parents. Although she did her best to charm them later, it was a case of* ***first impressions are the most lasting****; even after she married Mike they never did like her.* ♦ *You must dress smartly for the interview and think of some interesting questions to ask the interviewer about the company;* ***first impressions are the most lasting****.* ♦ *I discovered later that Bob is considered to be rather a dishonest man, but he was very helpful to me when I first met him and* ***first impressions are the most lasting****.*

First things first

The most important things must be dealt with first. This proverb is sometimes used humorously: ♦ *There are several matters that must be dealt with at the first meeting of the committee; but* ***first things first****, we must appoint a new chairperson.* ♦ *I know you've all got a lot of suggestions for the office party; but* ***first things first****, we must decide on a suitable date.* ♦ *Now that everyone is here, we can get on with the rehearsal; but* ***first things first****, let's all have a cup of tea.*

Fools rush in where angels fear to tread

People who have little experience or knowledge of a situation, and little tact, often act hastily and recklessly and attempt to deal with difficult or sensitive things which wiser, more experienced, or more tactful people would not: ♦ *We all know that Meg and Lucy are cousins as well as being good friends and that, when they have a row, it is best to keep out of it. But Alice is new to the area and started to intervene when they began arguing with each other, at which point they both started shouting at her;* ***fools rush in where angels fear to tread****.* ♦ *The situation between Sara and Tony is very sensitive just now, as they're trying to sort out their differences and save their relationship. Unfortunately, Mary, who is quite her tactless, has just asked them both when they are going to go out with other people;* ***fools rush in where angels fear to tread****.*

Did you know?

In origin, the proverb is a reference to a line in Alexander Pope's *Essay on Criticism* (1711). It is a very common proverb and is sometimes shortened to **fools rush in**, which has become a cliché:

♦ ***Fools rush in****; anyone with any sensitivity would have realized that Jenny was very upset about the news that she couldn't have children, but Polly started going on about how you can have a much better lifestyle without children.*

Forewarned is forearmed

Similar

Prevention is better than cure.

You are much more able to deal with a situation if you have some advance warning of it and can make any necessary preparations: ♦ *It's useful to know that one lane of the motorway is going to be closed at the weekend because we can make arrangements to leave on our trip on Friday;* ***forewarned is forearmed****.* ♦ *Our football coach has just discovered that the other team have appointed an extremely good striker. We had thought it was going to be an easy match, but* ***forewarned is forearmed****.* ♦ *I am glad we discovered that the council are contemplating reducing the opening hours of the local library;* ***forewarned is forearmed*** *and there is time to organize a protest movement.*

Four eyes see more than two

Similar

Two heads are better than one.

Opposite

Too many cooks spoil the broth.

Two people are more likely to notice something than one person is: ♦ *I wonder if you would help me look for my ring, which I've dropped on the sand;* ***four eyes see more than two****.* ♦ *The street is somewhere in this area of the map but the type is very small and my eyesight is not very good.* ***Four eyes see more than two****; so come and help me look.* ♦ *Please have a look at this financial statement; there's an error in it somewhere and* ***four eyes see more than two****.*

G

Give a dog a bad name and hang him

If a person once gets a bad reputation, people will always have a bad opinion of him, whether or not this is deserved and whether or not the person changes: ♦ *Tom is a very hard-working, honest young man. However, as a teenager, he was once in trouble with the police and now he is finding it very difficult to get a job;* ***give a dog a bad name and hang him****. ♦ Pam is a very caring sensible young woman who will be a wonderful wife and mother, but Phil's parents don't want him to marry her because they heard that she was rather wild when she was a young teenager. It was a long time ago,* ***but give a dog a bad name and hang him****. ♦ Sally was suffering from depression when she was arrested for shoplifting, but she feels that she will always be regarded as a thief in the town and is thinking of moving away; it's a case of* ***give a dog a bad name and hang him****.*

Help

This proverb is well known and, frequently, only the first part of it is used:

♦ *The PE teacher was accused of assaulting a pupil, and even though he was found not guilty of the charge, he felt that he had to leave his post because people were gossiping about him;* ***give a dog a bad name****.*

An alternative form of this proverb is **give a dog a bad name and you might as well hang him**:

♦ *The police held Bill for questioning in connection with the break-in at the factory. Although he had an alibi and the police said that they were satisfied that he had nothing to do with the crime, people are still treating him with suspicion;* ***give a dog a bad name and you might as well hang him****.*

Give a man enough rope and he will hang himself

If you give someone full scope and freedom to do as they wish, they will eventually do something which damages or destroys themselves: ♦ *I know that you're annoyed that your colleague does very little work and leaves you to do most of it. Still,* ***give a man enough rope and he will hang himself****; I've heard that the boss is becoming aware of the situation. ♦ The fact that the marketing manager is spending far too much on taking people out to expensive lunches will be noticed eventually;* ***give a man enough rope and he will hang himself****. ♦ Josh has been telling the boss a lot of lies in order to get time off work, but his last lie was so unlikely* *that the boss is beginning to get suspicious;* ***give a man enough rope and he will hang himself.***

Did you know?

An earlier, and now archaic, form of the proverb was **give a thief enough rope and he will hang himself**, a reference to the fact that thieving used to be punished by hanging.

Give credit where credit is due

Similar

Give the Devil his due.

You should acknowledge that someone has done well when they have done something which is worthy of praise, even if you do not like the person or even if they do not usually do something very well: ♦ *I don't think Jane's a very good manager, but* ***give credit where credit is due****—she handled that customer's complaint very tactfully.* ♦ *Usually Mary's essays are rather boring, but* ***give credit where credit is due****—this account of her travels overseas is very interesting.* ♦ *We thought that we would beat the other team easily and we did in fact win. However,* ***give credit where credit is due****, they played very well and it was a much more difficult game than we had been expecting.*

Give the Devil his due

Similar

Give credit where credit is due.

You should acknowledge that someone has done well or done something which is worthy of praise, even if you do not like the person or if he or she does not usually do good things: ♦ ***Give the Devil his due****; Meg is usually an incredibly mean person, but she gave a very generous donation to our local children's charity.* ♦ ***Give the Devil his due****; the team who beat us usually commit a good many fouls, but this time they played fairly and they deserved to win.* ♦ ***Give the Devil his due****; our next-door neighbour doesn't like children and usually shouts at ours. When our daughter fell in the street and cut her knee badly, our neighbour took the child into her house and bandaged the knee.*

God helps them that help themselves

This proverb is used to encourage a spirit of self-help in people: ♦ *The Jackson family are very religious and spend a lot of time praying to God to help them in their poverty-stricken situation. They should spend some time looking for work as well as praying;* ***God helps them that help themselves****.* ♦ *Bill and Patsy are complaining that fate dealt them a cruel blow when their landlord decided to sell the flat they live in. Perhaps they should remember that* ***God helps them that help themselves****; they could afford to buy a flat if they spent less money on clothes and on having a good time.* ♦ *The employment situation isn't very good in the country just now, but those people who really want to work can usually find it;* ***God helps them that help themselves****.*

Help

An alternative form of the proverb is **God helps those who help themselves**.

Good wine needs no bush

Something that is of high quality does not require to be advertised or promoted: ♦ *Tim says that he spends very little money on advertising his restaurant because people recommend it to each other and it's always full;* ***good wine needs no bush****.* ♦ *Jill owns a chain of small bakeries which sell wonderful cakes. You won't see large advertisements for them because* ***good wine needs no bush*** *and the cakes are always in great demand.* ♦ *Harry has never needed to pay for advertising for his two holiday cottages because the same people come year after year and tell friends about it;* ***good wine needs no bush****.*

Did you know?

Formerly, shops had a sign outside them to advertise the kind of goods they sold. In the case of wine shops, it was originally an ivy bush, since the ivy in ancient times was sacred to Bacchus, the god of wine in Greek mythology.

Great minds think alike

Clever people form the same opinions about things or make the same decisions. This proverb is often used humorously in self-congratulation or self-admiration when you have expressed the same opinion as someone else: ♦ *I had just suggested going to the zoo when Molly came in and made the same suggestion;* ***great minds think alike****.* ♦ *I had just proposed that we hire a car for the day and go for a drive in the country when Frank said that John had come up with the same idea just before I arrived;* ***great minds think alike****.* ♦ *Apparently Joe and Sara are looking for a house in the same area as we are;* ***great minds think alike****.*

Help

The proverb is sometimes shortened to **great minds**:
♦ *I've just heard that Ken and Jean have chosen the same hotel for their wedding reception as we have, although on a different day, of course;* ***great minds****.*

A popular reply to this proverb is '**Small minds seldom differ**' or '**Fools seldom differ**.'

Great oaks from little acorns grow

Often things that are large and successful begin in a small, insignificant way: ♦ *The Lewis family have just sold their textile business to a multinational company for a huge sum of money. The business was started by their great-grandfather in his front room;* ***great oaks from little acorns grow****.* ♦ *We need a great deal of money to make the necessary repairs to the church roof. If a lot of people come up with ideas which will make even a small amount of money, we'll reach our target eventually;* ***great oaks from little acorns grow****.* ♦ *The idea for a writers' conference was developed with just a few writers who lived locally having an informal get-together. Now it has become an important, international, annual event, attracting large numbers of writers from all over the world;* ***great oaks from little acorns grow****.*

Help

Other adjectives, such as 'mighty' and 'tall', are sometimes substituted for 'great'.

H

Half a loaf is better than no bread

A little of something, or something less than you want, is better than nothing and you should be grateful for what you have: ♦ *I'm going to have to share a room in the flat, which I don't want to do, but there is a severe lack of accommodation around here and* ***half a loaf is better than no bread****.* ♦ *Although our society had failed to get a bigger grant from the council, at least they gave us something;* ***half a loaf is better than no bread****.* ♦ *Peter is disappointed that the bank would not give him a bigger loan, but they did give him enough to start up his business and* ***half a loaf is better than no bread****.*

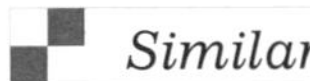

Something is better than nothing.

Handsome is as handsome does

Good looks are all very well, but they have their limitations and more is required of people than simply looking attractive. This proverb is rather old-fashioned: ♦ *Len's new wife is certainly very pretty and well dressed, but* ***handsome is as handsome does****, and Len needs someone who will look after his motherless children and help him in his shop.* ♦ *The new sales manager is undeniably good-looking, but* ***handsome is as handsome does****; he will have to be hard-working and energetic if he is going to improve the firm's sales figures.* ♦ *Mike says that we should be looking for an attractive young woman to be our hotel receptionist. But* ***handsome is as handsome does*** *and we also need someone who will be polite and friendly to guests, be a good administrator and be able to use their own initiative.*

Help

Originally, 'handsome' referred to chivalrous or polite behaviour.

He that goes a-borrowing goes a-sorrowing

This is a warning that borrowing money is not a good idea because such action will end in regret or disaster: ♦ *Sally has a whole series of credit cards and, now that she has lost her job, she cannot possibly make the required monthly repayments;* ***he that goes a-borrowing goes a-sorrowing****.* ♦ *Ben, knowing that Rose had fallen in love with the house, borrowed far more than they could afford in order to buy it, and now the bank is threatening to repossess the house;* ***he that goes a-borrowing goes a-sorrowing****.*

He travels fastest who travels alone

Someone who is alone and has no companions or dependants to take into consideration is likely to make more progress in life and be more successful: ♦ *We need someone for this job who is able to go anywhere in the world at a moment's notice. It is only suitable for those who believe that* ***he travels fastest who travels alone****, and not for people with families.* ♦ *As far as Liz is concerned, it has always been a case of* ***he travels fastest who travels alone****. When she left university, she said that she would rather have a brilliant career than a husband and family, and she has never changed her mind.* ♦ *At the moment, Christopher isn't interested in marriage or a serious relationship with any of his girlfriends because he thinks that that would interfere with his ambitious career plans. He is firmly of the opinion that* ***he travels fastest who travels alone****.*

He who fights and runs away, may live to fight another day

This proverb points out the advantage of being cautious and prudent and of conserving your energy for another occasion: ♦ *At the first protest meeting, we soon realized that we did not have enough information about the proposed new housing estate and so we brought it quickly to a close and went off to gather more data;* ***he who fights and runs away, may live to fight another day.*** ♦ *We were heavily outnumbered by the enemy forces and, after the first skirmish, we decided to retreat until we could meet up with more of our army;* ***he who fights and runs away, may live to fight another day.***

Similar

Discretion is the better part of valour.

He who hesitates is lost

This is a warning against indecision since failing to act might result in failure to achieve what you want: ♦ *If you are interested in the job that is advertised, send in a letter of application right away. I think a lot of people will be interested in it and* ***he who hesitates is lost.*** ♦ *Emma wasn't sure if she wanted to play in the club tennis team or not and she said that she would let them know. But it was a case of* ***he who hesitates is lost****; by the time she had decided that she did want to be a member of the team, they had given the place to someone else.* ♦ *If you are interested in Jenny, you should ask her out right away because she's very attractive and other people are bound to want to go out with her;* ***he who hesitates is lost.***

Opposite

Look before you leap.

Second thoughts are best.

He who laughs last, laughs longest

The person who wins the final victory at the end of something has more reason to celebrate than someone who has had a minor victory in the course of something. This is a warning not to express delight at victory too soon: ♦ *Our opponents' fans were sure that they had won and were singing victory songs when one of our strikers scored two goals in the closing minutes of the game;* ***he who laughs last, laughs longest****.* ♦ *Tom was absolutely sure that he would win the tennis final because he had won all his previous matches easily and his opponent was very inexperienced. After a hard-fought match, he lost and everyone congratulated the winner;* ***he who laughs last, laughs longest****.*

Help

An earlier, and now less common, form of this proverb is **he laughs best who laughs last**. The idiom **have the last laugh** has been formed from the proverb:

♦ *Ken's rival candidate was gloating when the early indications were that he was winning the election. But when all the votes were counted, Ken's supporters had* ***the last laugh****; he had won easily.*

He who pays the piper calls the tune

The person who is providing the money for a project has a right to be involved in deciding how it will be spent: ♦ *If the boss is providing the wine for the party, I think you should ask him if he wants a say in choosing it;* ***he who calls the piper plays the tune****.* ♦ *Mr Young, a local businessman, is providing most of the money for the new community hall and he has asked to see the plans for it, which seems reasonable;* ***he who pays the piper calls the tune****, as they say.* ♦ *Mrs Smart has kindly offered to pay for flowers to decorate the hall for the charity ball and I think we should ask her if she has any preferences for any particular flowers;* ***he who pays the piper calls the tune****.*

Help

This is a very common proverb and both parts of it are commonly used as idioms:

♦ *It's time that the public were given more information on government spending; after all, as taxpayers,* ***we pay the piper****.* ♦ *The owners of the factory say that they are paying* *the workers' wages and that* ***they should be calling the tune*** *when decisions about production schedules are made.*

Did you know?

In origin, the proverb refers to the fact that musicians used to travel around playing, as requested, for dancers or those wishing to be entertained, and the person who paid the musician chose the tunes which were played.

He who sups with the Devil should have a long spoon

If you are going to associate with bad or cunning people, you will have to be very careful: ♦ *John should be very cautious if he is planning to do business with Jeff because Jeff has been involved in some dishonest dealings;* ***he who sups with the Devil should have a long spoon****.* ♦ *Anne ought to be very careful in her dealings with Brian and, above all, she ought not to lend him any money;* ***he who sups with the Devil should have a long spoon****.* ♦ *The local antique dealer is suspected of receiving stolen goods and you should be wary about what you buy from him;* ***he who sups with the Devil should have a long spoon****.*

Hell hath no fury like a woman scorned

A woman who is rejected by a man is likely to be extremely angry and to seek revenge: ♦ *Joan cut the arms off all her husband's jackets and shirts when he left her for another woman;* ***hell hath no fury like a woman scorned****.* ♦ *When Frank walked off with another woman, his wife burned all his business papers and books in a bonfire in the back garden;* ***hell hath no fury like a woman scorned****.* ♦ *Jack had a very valuable collection of old stamps, but his wife gave the collection away for nothing when he left home;* ***hell hath no fury like a woman scorned****.*

Similar

Revenge is sweet.

Help

This proverb is also found in the shortened form **hell has no fury**:

♦ *When Grace found out about her husband's infidelity, she deliberately crashed his expensive car into a wall;* ***hell has no fury***.

Did you know?

The proverb is an adaptation of lines from *The Mourning Bride* (1697), a play by William Congreve—'Heaven has no rage, like love to hatred turned, nor Hell a fury like a woman scorned.' As well as meaning great anger, the word 'fury' was also applied in classical mythology to three goddesses who took terrible vengeance on wrongdoers and punished crime.

History repeats itself

If something happens once it is likely to happen again. The proverb is often used of something which happens in a particular family: ♦ *Harry was sent to prison as a very young man and now his 20-year-old son has just been given a jail sentence;* ***history repeats itself***. ♦ *Almost exactly ten years ago there was a major fire in that garment factory;* ***history repeats itself***. ♦ *Lucy married a man who was much older than herself and now her daughter has done the same thing;* ***history repeats itself***.

Home is where the heart is

Similar

East, west, home is best.

The place which you call home is the place where your loved ones are or the place where you want to be, because you love it: ♦ *John has lived in America for several years, but all his family are still in London and he still thinks of the city as home;* ***home is where the heart is***. ♦ *When Mary went on holiday to Australia, she married a sheep farmer and now thinks of the country as home;* ***home is where the heart is***.

Honesty is the best policy

This proverb emphasizes the importance of truthfulness and integrity: ♦ *I think you should tell Sara that you damaged her car in an accident while she was away, even though you have had it repaired;* ***honesty is the best policy****.* ♦ *Dan made the right decision when he decided to tell the head teacher that he had broken the window. He might easily have got away with it, but* ***honesty is the best policy****.* ♦ *It's a very bad idea to tell lies about your qualifications and experience in a job application;* ***honesty is the best policy****, even if you don't get the job.*

Similar

Confession is good for the soul.

Honey catches more flies than vinegar

You are more likely to influence or persuade people if you use friendly, soothing, sympathetic, flattering language than if you use sharp, unfriendly, angry language: ♦ *The management team has a new leader and he obviously has decided that* ***honey catches more flies than vinegar*** *when it comes to negotiating with the workers' representatives.* ♦ *Patsy is anxious to get the other members of the committee to agree with her decision. Unfortunately, she is causing hostility by trying to bully them instead of trying to charm and cajole them; she should learn that* ***honey catches more flies than vinegar****.* ♦ *The students in that class have a bad reputation and teachers who have to teach them usually decide to treat them very sternly. Yet the new teacher seems to be able to control them without raising her voice; it must be the case that* ***honey catches more flies than vinegar****.*

Hope for the best and prepare for the worst

Whilst you should hope that something will have a good or fortunate outcome, this may not come about and you should also make preparations for dealing with a bad or unfortunate outcome: ♦ *It's a case of* ***hope for the best and prepare for the worst****; we are optimistic that our bid will be accepted for the house, but if it isn't we're going to put our furniture in store and move in with my parents until we find another house.* ♦ *I've decided to* ***hope for the best and prepare for the worst****; I think it's possible that I have passed the exams, but just in case I haven't, I have put my name down for some revision courses.* ♦ ***Hope for the best and prepare for the worst****; you may well not be one of those people who are declared redundant when the firm is taken over, but you should start looking for another job in case you are.*

Help

This proverb is sometimes shortened to **hope for the best**.

Hope springs eternal

Similar

A drowning man will clutch at a straw.

While there's life, there's hope.

People are always inclined to hope, even in the most desperate situations: ♦ *The family have been told that their grandfather is likely to die before the end of the week, but some of them believe that the doctors have made a mistake;* ***hope springs eternal****.* ♦ *The hill-walkers have now been on the mountains for three nights in the worst blizzards that have ever hit the area. Although experts say that no one could survive in such conditions without proper mountaineering equipment, the wives of the hill-walkers seem convinced that they will be all right;* ***hope springs eternal****.* ♦ *Bob admits that he did very little work for the exam and could answer hardly any questions, but amazingly he's still of the opinion that he might pass;* ***hope springs eternal****.*

Help

This proverb is very common and has become a cliché. It is also found, less commonly, in the original, longer version **hope springs eternal in the human**

breast. This is a reference to lines from Alexander Pope's *Essay on Man* (1732): 'Hope springs eternal in the human breast. Man never is, but always to be blest.'

Hunger is the best sauce

If you are hungry, all food tastes delicious, however plain and simple: ♦ *The bread and cheese which were given to us at the end of our long walk tasted absolutely wonderful;* ***hunger is the best sauce.*** ♦ *It's a waste of time cooking anything fancy for my son and his friends when they come back from the football match. The reason is that they'll be so ravenous they won't notice what they're eating;* ***hunger is the best sauce.*** ♦ *The children are fussy eaters and you should tell them that, if they don't eat the food which you put in front of them, they are not getting anything else;* ***hunger is the best sauce.***

I

If a thing's worth doing, it's worth doing well

If you want to achieve anything worthwhile, you have to be prepared to put effort into it and do it properly: ♦ *If you're going to apply for the job you should type out your CV in a professional manner;* ***if a thing's worth doing, it's worth doing well.*** ♦ *If we're going to have a dinner party we should give some thought to the table decoration as well as to the food and drink;* ***if a thing's worth doing, it's worth doing well.*** ♦ *I've asked a few friends round to celebrate my birthday and I was just going to buy some drinks and crisps. But my mother says that* ***if a thing's worth doing, it's worth doing well,*** *and is insisting on preparing some food and decorating the room.*

Similar

Don't spoil the ship for a ha'porth of tar.

Help

An alternative form of this proverb is **if a job's worth doing, it's worth doing well**.

If the blind lead the blind, both shall fall into the ditch

If the people who are in charge of a venture know as little as the people whom they are supposed to be guiding or instructing, then the venture is going to fail.

Help

The proverb is not often used in its complete form nowadays, but the phrase **the blind leading the blind** is very commonly used to emphasize the lack of knowledge or lack of ability of someone in charge and has become a cliché:

♦ *The teacher who has been asked to teach the students about modern art admits to knowing very little about the subject; it will be a case of the* ***blind leading the blind****.* ♦ *Sally says that she is going to teach her daughter to cook, but Sally is one of the worst cooks I know; certainly it will be the* ***blind leading the blind****.* ♦ *I'll certainly act as your guide, but it may be a case of the* ***blind leading the blind****; I haven't visited this city for many years.*

Another proverb which relates blindness to ignorance is **in the country of the blind, the one-eyed man is king**.

Did you know?

This proverb has a biblical origin, being a reference to Matthew 15:14—'Let them alone; they be blind leaders of the blind. And if the blind lead the blind, both shall fall into the ditch.'

If the cap fits, wear it

If a description which has been given, or a remark which has been made, is applicable to you, then acknowledge this to be the case. This proverb is often used to indicate to someone that a criticism made of them is accurate or fair: ♦ *Fred said that he hoped Jenny wasn't referring to him when she said that there were some very untrustworthy people around, but she replied, '**If the cap fits, wear it**.'* ♦ *Jack said that only a fool would believe what Fred had said and, when Sally asked if he was suggesting that she was foolish, Jack replied, '**If the cap fits, wear it**.'*

Help

This proverb is often shortened to **if the cap fits**, which has become a cliché:

♦ *Janet said that most of her friends were cowards and, when John asked if that included him, she said, '**If the cap fits**.'*

A much less well-known version is **if the shoe fits**.

Did you know?

In origin, the proverb is thought to refer to a dunce's cap.

If you play with fire, you get burnt

If you take risks, you will get hurt or damaged in some way: ♦ *Joe had taken to placing substantial bets on horses and it was only a matter of time before he lost a great deal of money; **if you play with fire, you get burnt**.* ♦ *Martin put a lot of his money into high-risk investments and suffered considerable losses when some of them failed; still, **if you play with fire, you get burnt**.* ♦ *We all told Julie that Frank was a crook but she persisted in inviting him to stay in her house and he stole her money and jewellery; **if you play with fire, you get burnt**.*

Help

The phrase **play with fire** is also very commonly used and has become a cliché:

♦ *Sally knew that she was **playing with fire** by having an affair with her boss, but she said that she loved him very much.*

Ignorance is bliss

Similar

What the eye doesn't see, the heart doesn't grieve over.

What you don't know can't hurt you.

There are situations in which it is better not to know about something: ♦ *Jean seemed genuinely unaware that her youngest son was a rogue. Although several of her friends knew what he was really like, they decided not to tell her on the grounds that* ***ignorance is bliss****.* ♦ *Beth has a feeling that her husband's business dealings are not completely honest, but she believes that* ***ignorance is bliss*** *and does not ask him any questions about it.* ♦ *The antique dealer thought that the table might be stolen property, but it was undoubtedly a bargain and he decided not to make any investigations; it was a case of* ***ignorance is bliss****.*

Help

This proverb is a very commonly used and has become a cliché. It has given rise to the phrase **blissful ignorance**:

♦ *Everyone knew that her daughter was stealing from her, but Joan remained in* ***blissful ignorance****.*

Did you know?

The original form of the proverb was **where ignorance is bliss, 'tis folly to be wise**:

♦ ***Where ignorance is bliss, 'tis folly to be wise*** *and I would rather not know the details of the boss's tax affairs.*

The longer proverb is a reference to a poem entitled 'Ode on a Distant Prospect of Eton College' (1742) by Thomas Gray—'Thought would destroy their paradise. No more; where ignorance is bliss, 'tis folly to be wise.'

Ignorance of the law is no excuse for breaking it

The fact that you were unaware of the existence of a law, rule or regulation does not excuse you for not acting in accordance with it: ♦ *Bob tried to tell the policeman that he did not know what the speed limit was in that area when he was stopped for speeding, but the policeman refused to accept his excuse;* ***ignorance of the***

law is no excuse for breaking it. ♦ *Bert was a new member of the club and he said that he hadn't realized that he had to enter the names of his guests in a book. He ought to have read the rule book and, in any case,* ***ignorance of the law is no excuse for breaking it***. ♦ *I know that* ***ignorance of the law is no excuse for breaking it****, but we had no idea that the children were not allowed to play football in that park. There is only one small notice at one of the entries and we did not see it.*

Help

The proverb is sometimes shortened to **ignorance of the law is no excuse**.

Imitation is the sincerest form of flattery

Someone who admires another person very much often shows this admiration by copying that person's mannerisms, actions, clothes, etc: ♦ *As soon as Elizabeth buys a new outfit, Sara gets one very similar to it, if not identical. They say that* ***imitation is the sincerest form of flattery****, but Elizabeth is getting very tired of the situation.* ♦ *Jane spent a lot of money getting a trendy new hairstyle at an expensive salon in the city and was upset to discover that two of her friends then went and got their hair done in a similar style at the local hairdresser's. We tried to tell her that* ***imitation is the sincerest form of flattery****, but she wouldn't listen.* ♦ *We have just visited Tom and Anne in their new house and we were amazed to see that it is decorated exactly like ours. My husband said that* ***imitation is the sincerest form of flattery****, but I think that they should have come up with their own ideas, instead of copying ours.*

In for a penny, in for a pound

This proverb is used to indicate that you are committed to a course of action and are prepared to

Similar

One might as well be hanged for a sheep as a lamb.

take the risk, or spend the money or resources, that this involves until the action is completed: ♦ *We hadn't realized how long it would take us to do a tour of the islands, because of the infrequency and unreliability of the ferry services. However, we were determined to finish the trip;* ***in for a penny, in for a pound****.* ♦ *When Harry bought the house, he didn't appreciate quite how much work would have to be done before it was habitable. Now he's decided that it's a case of* ***in for a penny, in for a pound*** *and has borrowed money in order to carry out a complete renovation.* ♦ *I was only going to buy a new dress for Jill's wedding, but it made my jacket, shoes and handbag look very shabby and I replaced these as well; it was* ***in for a penny, in for a pound****. Now I have very little money left to buy a wedding present.*

In the country of the blind, the one-eyed man is king

Someone who knows very little about something can appear to be very knowledgeable, if the other people involved are even more ignorant: ♦ *When I joined the local chess club, I thought that all the rest of the players would be experts, but it's a new club for beginners and I'm the best player;* ***in the country of the blind, the one-eyed man is king****.* ♦ *Sue usually does the cooking when she and her flatmates ask people to dinner. She's not a good cook and the food is usually inedible, but the others are even worse and* ***in the country of the blind, the one-eyed man is king***. For comparison, see **if the blind lead the blind, both shall fall into the ditch**.

It is best to be on the safe side

Similar

Better be safe than sorry.

It is best to be cautious and prudent and not to take unnecessary risks: ♦ *I don't think the child's illness is anything to worry about, but* ***it is better to be on the safe side*** *and take her to the doctor.* ♦ *There shouldn't be much traffic on the roads so early in the morning, but*

***it is best to be on the safe side** and allow at least an hour to get to the airport.* ♦ *It doesn't look as though the recent spring gales have done any damage to the roof, but **it is better to be on the safe side** and I am going to get a roofer to check it.*

Discretion is the better part of valour.

It is better to be born lucky than rich

It is better to be born the kind of person who always seems to enjoy good luck than to be born wealthy, presumably because if you are born lucky, it is likely that you will be lucky enough to make money as well as to achieve other things: ♦ *My mother always used to say '**It is better to be born lucky than rich**'; although I'm quite lucky at some things, this doesn't extend to making money.* ♦ *The Lee sisters come from a very poor family, but they have all been very successful; one of the three said recently that they have all enjoyed good luck all their lives and that **it is better to be born lucky than rich**.*

It is better to give than to receive

This proverb emphasizes the advantages of giving: ♦ *Children love getting presents so much that it is sometimes difficult to teach them that **it is better to give than to receive**.* ♦ *I don't think that Helen believes in the saying '**It is better to give than to receive**' because she always expects gifts of expensive jewellery from her many boyfriends, but gives them cheap ties and socks in return.* ♦ *They say that **it is better to give than to receive**, but most of us still love receiving gifts and unwrapping them.*

Did you know?

The proverb is a version of a quotation from Acts 20:35 in the Bible: 'It is more blessed to give than to receive.'

It is easier to pull down than to build up

It is easier to destroy or criticize something than to construct, create or do something: ♦ *During the 1960s, the city council gave permission for a lot of beautiful old buildings to be razed to the ground and these were replaced with some really ugly buildings, which are now an eyesore;* **it is easier to pull down than to build up**. ♦ *The new government is busy doing away with the previous government's strategies for the economy, but we haven't heard what their own plans are;* **it is easier to pull down than to build up**. ♦ *Paul says that his brother became a theatre critic after having tried unsuccessfully to write plays himself;* **it is easier to pull down than to build up**.

It is easy to be wise after the event

Similar

It is too late to lock the stable door after the horse has bolted.

Once something has happened, and all the facts are known, it is easy to see what has gone wrong and how it should have been dealt with: ♦ *After Mike was attacked in his own home, Paul said that it was obvious that the boy was violent and that Mike should not have invited him to stay with him. But* **it is easy to be wise after the event** *and the boy was the nephew of Mike's oldest friends, with no history of violent behaviour.* ♦ *When Meg had a nervous breakdown, Julie said that she had thought for some time that there was something wrong with her. Still,* **it is easy to be wise after the event**, *and Julie had never said anything to Meg's friends, who all thought that she was coping well with a difficult situation.* ♦ *We really shouldn't have bought this house, because it will cost far more than we can afford to renovate it.* **It is easy to be wise after the event** *and we didn't realize until after we moved in what a bad state it's in.*

It is never too late to learn

See **you are never too old to learn**.

It is the first step that is difficult

Beginning a project or task is often the most difficult part of it: ♦ *I really must start writing my history essay tonight and then it won't seem such an impossible task;* ***it is the first step that is difficult.*** ♦ *It's hard to give up smoking, but you'll feel better after a week or two;* ***it is the first step that is difficult.*** ♦ *It's understandable that Beth still feels sad about the death of her husband, but she should try to get out and meet new people, rather than staying at home all the time;* ***it is the first step that is difficult.***

Similar

Well begun is half done.

A good beginning makes a good ending.

Help

Another form of this proverb is **the first step is the hardest**.

It is the last straw that breaks the camel's back

This proverb suggests that it is the last one of a series of problems or burdens which, after all the others, finally makes it impossible for someone or something to tolerate a situation: ♦ *We loved the house, but a great many things had gone wrong with it, such as the plumbing and the central heating. When the roof needed major repairs,* ***it was the last straw that broke the camel's back****; we decided to move.* ♦ *Pam's boss was always criticizing her unjustly and usually she didn't say anything. Yesterday he accused her again, quite wrongly, of being late and* ***it was the last straw that broke the camel's back****; Pam lost her temper with him and resigned.* ♦ *Tom's firm was not in good financial shape, but he thought that he could keep it going until the market improved. Then he received an unexpectedly high tax bill—****it was the last straw that broke the camel's back****—and the firm had to close down.*

Help

The proverb is sometimes shortened to **the last straw** and used idiomatically. Used this way, it has become a cliché:

♦ *We were tired of Lucy's constant complaining and when she complained about having to sit in the back of the car, it was* ***the last straw****; we told her to find her own way home.* ♦ *Mary and Mark were having money problems and the increase in interest rates was* ***the last straw****. They had to sell their house to pay off their debts.*

It is too late to lock the stable door after the horse has bolted

Similar

It is easy to be wise after the event.

There is no point in taking action to prevent something from happening after it has already happened: ♦ *As soon as her house was broken into, Mary immediately had a burglar alarm installed. I was tempted to tell her that* ***it was too late to lock the stable door after the horse had bolted****.* ♦ *After a small fire started in her kitchen, Sally installed a series of smoke alarms in her house. When Pete said that* ***it was too late to lock the stable door after the horse had bolted****, she replied that she was taking action against possible future fires.* ♦ *Jim started training very hard after he unexpectedly lost the tennis final, but his coach simply commented that* ***it was too late to lock the stable door after the horse had bolted****.*

Help

An alternative form of the proverb is **it is too late to lock the stable door after the horse has gone**. Either 'close' or 'shut' is sometimes substituted for 'lock' in both forms of the proverb, for example, **it is too late to shut the stable door after the horse has bolted**. Part of the proverb is commonly used as an idiom:

♦ *The number of police officers in the town centre was increased after the spate of attacks on women, but several women's groups said that it was a case of* ***locking the stable door after the horse had bolted****.*

It never rains but it pours

One misfortune always seems to be followed by others: ♦ *First the central heating system had to be replaced and then we discovered dry rot in the attic;* ***it never rains but it pours****.* ♦ *First our eldest child broke his leg and then the twins developed mumps;* ***it never rains but it pours****.* ♦ *Today at the office, my computer crashed, I spilt coffee on my white blouse and I had to deal with an extremely rude customer;* ***it never rains but it pours****.*

Similar

Misfortunes never come singly.

It takes all sorts to make a world

We must accept the fact that society is inevitably made up of many different kinds of people who vary greatly in their opinions, attitudes or habits: ♦ *The rest of the family love living in the city, but our youngest son has decided to go and live on a remote, sparsely populated island;* ***it takes all sorts to make a world****.* ♦ *When Miss Jones first moved into the area, all the neighbours invited her to various social occasions, but she turned them all down and seemed to prefer her own company; ah well,* ***it takes all sorts to make a world****.* ♦ *I don't understand Jack because although he has plenty of money he lives in a broken-down house and wears very shabby clothes; still,* ***it takes all sorts to make a world****.*

Similar

Live and let live.

Variety is the spice of life.

Help

The proverb is frequently shortened to **it takes all sorts** and, in this form, it has become a cliché:

♦ *We invited Meg to come on a cruise with us, but she said that she preferred to stay at home;* ***it takes all sorts****, I suppose.*

It takes two to make a bargain

There cannot be a bargain unless two people agree to it and keep it: ♦ *Peter thought that he had made a bargain with Mark to buy his car, but Mark has now sold the car to someone else;* ***it takes two to make a bargain****.* ♦ *We tried to come to an agreement with our neighbour to buy a part of his garden, but he wasn't* *keen on the idea and* ***it takes two to make a bargain****.* ♦ *Ken is interested in buying Sally's flat, but the price is too high for him and she won't reduce it;* ***it takes two to make a bargain****.*

Did you know?

The earlier, now archaic, form of this proverb was **there are two words to every bargain**.

It takes two to make a quarrel

Similar

It takes two to tango.

This proverb emphasizes the obvious point that one person alone cannot quarrel: ♦ *Bert puts all the blame on Joe for starting the family feud, but* ***it takes two to make a quarrel****.* ♦ *Jane and Molly are not speaking to each other and Molly says that it's all Jane's fault, but* ***it takes two to make a quarrel****.* ♦ *Pat is trying to get Julie to be friends with Len again, but Julie has refused, saying the quarrel was caused by Len in the first place; however,* ***it takes two to make a quarrel****.*

It takes two to tango

Similar

It takes two to make a quarrel.

This proverb is used, with reference to a situation which involves two people or groups, to indicate that both are responsible for it: ♦ *Jane blames Mark for their quarrel, but Jane must bear some of the responsibility because* ***it takes two to tango****.* ♦ *The union have said that they are anxious to come to an agreement with management but that* ***it takes two to tango****, and management is being uncooperative.* ♦ *We would have liked to settle the issue out of court, but the other side would not agree, and* ***it takes two to tango****.*

Did you know?

The tango is a dance of Latin-American origin and performed by two people.

It's a long lane that has no turning

This proverb is used to comfort people who are experiencing a period of misfortune by reminding them that it cannot go on forever: ♦ *Jim is having a miserable time just now—having lost his job and having been ill. But* ***it's a long lane that has no turning*** *and it looks as though his situation is beginning to improve.* ♦ *Harry suffered one misfortune after another and, for a long time, nothing seemed to go right for him.* ***It's a long lane that has no turning*** *and now he has a good job and is happily married with two children.*

It's an ill bird that fouls its own nest

Only a very bad or nasty person would do something that would harm his family and close friends or would say critical or bad things about them: ♦ *Jack must be a real rogue to have got his sister to invest money in a company which he knew was unstable;* ***it's an ill bird that fouls its own nest.*** ♦ *Several members of Jill's family have broken the law and most of them are lazy and idle. She is always ready to defend them if anyone criticizes them, and rightly so;* ***it's an ill bird that fouls its own nest.*** ♦ *Beth really should not tell her friends all about her husband's faults;* ***it's an ill bird that fouls its own nest.***

It's an ill wind that blows nobody any good

There is usually someone who benefits from a situation, however much of a misfortune or disadvantage the situation might be for other people: ♦ *People with mortgages or bank loans are horrified by the sudden large increase in the bank rate, but people with savings are delighted;* ***it's an ill wind that blows nobody any good.*** ♦ *It was unfortunate for Mary that she had to cancel her holiday at the last minute*

Similar

Every cloud has a silver lining.

One man's loss is another man's gain.

because of work commitments. But she had to pay the rent of the cottage anyway, and her sister and her family, who are too poor to afford a holiday, were able to have it free; ***it's an ill wind that blows nobody any good****.* ♦ *It's bad luck for Joe and his family that he is being transferred to a branch of the firm at the other side of the country for several months. However, it means that we can rent their house until we can find one to buy;* ***it's an ill wind that blows nobody any good****.*

Did you know?

The proverb has its origin in sailing in the days when all ships were powered by the wind.

It's no use crying over spilt milk

Similar

What's done cannot be undone.

There is no point in spending time in regretting or worrying about something that you cannot undo or change, however sorry you are: ♦ *It's terrible that your purse has been stolen, but don't let it spoil your holiday;* ***it's no use crying over spilt milk****.* ♦ *I know you're upset that your house plants died when you were away, but* ***it's no use crying over spilt milk****.* ♦ *It's very unfortunate that your application for the job was delayed in the post and arrived too late to be considered, but* ***it's no use crying over spilt milk*** *and you already have a very good job.*

Help

The proverb sometimes takes the form **it's no good crying over spilt milk**.

J

Judge not, that ye be not judged

This proverb urges people not to criticize or condemn other people or they themselves will be criticized or condemned: ♦ *When she was childless, Sara was always* *very critical of the behaviour of her friends' children. Now that she has very wild and rowdy twin boys, her friends take great delight in passing critical comments; she should have remembered the old proverb '**Judge not, that ye be not judged**.'* ♦ *It is a classic example of **judge not, that ye be not judged**; Alan is a driving instructor who's always lecturing his friends about their bad driving habits and he has just been fined for speeding.*

K

Know thyself

This proverb advises people to get to know all about themselves: ♦ ***Know thyself**; you could easily do that job if you put your mind to it.* ♦ *John blames Anne for the break-up of their relationship and seems quite unaware that his own behaviour was a major factor; it is a classic case of **know thyself**.* ♦ *Sue is a psychiatrist who spends all her working life trying to understand other people and their problems. Yet she seems to have very little insight when it comes to her own problems; it is a definite case of **know thyself**.*

Knowledge is power

If you know a lot about someone or something, that knowledge can give you power or control over them: ♦ *Tom has been with the firm a long time and knows quite a lot of secret information about the family who own it; **knowledge is power** and they are never likely to sack him.* ♦ *Mr Smart's secretary is the most highly paid in the company and the rumour is that she is paid a lot so that she will not tell people about his many extramarital affairs; **knowledge is power**.* ♦ *We are trying to gather as much data about the firm as possible before putting in a bid to take it over; **knowledge is power**.*

L

Laugh and the world laughs with you; weep and you weep alone

If you are happy or joyful everyone is quite happy to share in your emotion, but this is not true of sadness or misery: ♦ *Molly was miserable and alone when news of her divorce came through. She remembered how she had been surrounded by friends on the day of her wedding and thought of the old proverb* ***'Laugh and the world laughs with you; weep and you weep alone.'*** ♦ *Fred had failed the exam and none of his friends had come near him, being too busy celebrating the success of those who had passed. It was a case of* ***laugh and the world laughs with you; weep and you weep alone****.*

Help

This is a common proverb, and sometimes only the first half of it is used:

♦ *I was feeling depressed after a bad day at work and none of my friends wanted to go for a drink;* ***laugh and the world laughs with you****, as they say.*

Least said, soonest mended

The less you say, the less you can be blamed for or have to feel sorry about: ♦ *Our new neighbour's dog was digging up part of my garden, but I decided not to complain in case it started a feud;* ***least said, soonest mended****.* ♦ *I wouldn't bother arguing with Jim if I were you;* ***least said, soonest mended****, and he gets very aggressive in arguments.* ♦ *I was very angry and felt like telling Harry exactly what I thought of his appalling behaviour, but when I cooled down, I decided to say nothing;* ***least said, soonest mended****, and he did apologize.*

Leave well alone

You should not try to improve a situation or disturb it in any way if it is fine or acceptable as it is: ♦ *The present exam system has worked very well for several years, but the new head teacher seems determined to change it. I hope that he soon learns to* ***leave well alone****.* ♦ ***Leave well alone****; I know that you are longing to reorganize the filing system, but you are only working here temporarily and the secretary knows exactly where everything is.* ♦ *You should* ***leave well alone*** *instead of offering advice to Mary on how to feed her children; the children seem very healthy and Mary is likely to be offended.*

Help

An alternative form of this proverb is **let well alone**.

Similar

Let sleeping dogs lie.

Lend your money and lose your friend

This proverb is a warning not to lend money to a friend, as the money might not be repaid and this could result in the loss of your friendship: ♦ *Ken is a good friend but he is completely unreliable. You should not let him borrow money from you;* ***lend your money and lose your friend****, as they say.* ♦ *Mark and Ron were good friends for many years until Mark lent Ron some money to start a business which failed. As far as Mark was concerned, it was a case of* ***lend your money and lose your friend****.* ♦ *Mary wants me to lend her some money to pay for her holiday, but it's rather a lot and I'm afraid that she may not be able to repay it. I don't want it to be a case of* ***lend your money and lose your friend****.*

Similar

Neither a borrower nor a lender be.

Let sleeping dogs lie

Don't interfere with a potentially difficult or troublesome situation or person, if there is no trouble at present. This proverb is a warning not to look for trouble: ♦ *Beth made no reference to the quarrel*

Similar

Leave well alone.

which she had had with James and I wondered if I should mention it, but I decided to **let sleeping dogs lie**. ♦ *The council had not heard anything recently from the protest group and so they decided not to inform them of recent developments in the building programme, thinking it best to* **let sleeping dogs lie**. ♦ *John's neighbours constantly find things to complain about, but they have been surprisingly silent recently. John's policy is always to* **let sleeping dogs lie** *and he is avoiding his neighbours as much as possible.*

Did you know?

In origin, the proverb refers to a sleeping dog, such as a watchdog, which might be angry if it is awakened.

Let the cobbler stick to his last

Similar

Every man to his trade.

People should concentrate on what they are qualified to do and leave other things to those who are qualified to do them: ♦ *Ken wants to save money and redecorate the house himself, but Liz says that they should employ a professional decorator; she believes in the saying '***Let the cobbler stick to his last***' and Ken is not very good at decorating.* ♦ *DIY (Do-it-yourself) can be very dangerous, especially where electricity is involved; unless you really know what you're doing, it's better to* **let the cobbler stick to his last** *and employ a professional electrician.* ♦ *Emma insisted on trying to make her wedding dress herself, but it was just a waste of expensive material and she had to buy more material and employ a dressmaker; she should have* **let the cobbler stick to his last** *from the start.*

Let well alone

See **leave well alone**.

Lightning never strikes twice in the same place

Opposite

Misfortunes never come singly.

People are never affected by the same kind of trouble or misfortune more than once: ♦ *It's not true that* ***lightning never strikes twice in the same place****: Jean's son was killed in a car accident last year, just two years after her husband suffered a similar fate.* ♦ *Ben is hoping that* ***lightning never strikes twice in the same place****; he was declared redundant three years ago and now the firm that he is working for is in financial trouble.* ♦ *People are foolish to believe that* ***lightning never strikes twice in the same place****, as Jim knows only too well; both his first wife and his second wife died of breast cancer.*

Help

Another form of the proverb is **lightning never strikes the same place twice**.

Did you know?

It is, in fact, not true that lightning never strikes twice in the same place, whether literally or metaphorically. Exceptionally high buildings or trees are particularly susceptible to being hit by lightning.

Like father, like son

This is a reference to the fact that a man's or a boy's attitude or behaviour is very similar to that of his father: ♦ *I saw Peter losing his temper with his neighbour the other night;* ***like father, like son****, Peter's father couldn't tolerate that neighbour either.* ♦ *Ken's son Bob has just been charged with drink-driving;* ***like father, like son****, Ken used to drive home roaring drunk.* ♦ *Bill's father committed suicide and now Bill is suffering from clinical depression. His family are worried in case it will be a case of* ***like father, like son****.*

Help

An alternative version of this proverb is **like mother, like daughter**:

♦ *Mary's mother was a single parent and now Mary is doing an excellent job of bringing up her children on her own;* ***like mother, like daughter****.*

Like mother, like daughter

See **like father, like son**.

Like will to like

Similar

Birds of a feather flock together.

A man is known by the company he keeps.

People who are like each other in some way or have something in common with each other often associate with each other: ♦ *The new boy seems to be rather wild and has instantly formed a friendship with two of the worst-behaved boys in the school; teachers are afraid that it is a case of* ***like will to like****.* ♦ *It was* ***like will to like****; Jill and Ron are both extrovert, fun-loving people and they started going out together regularly almost as soon as they met.* ♦ *It's a case of* ***like will to like****; the gang consists of all the rowdiest youths in the community.*

Little pitchers have big ears

Similar

Walls have ears.

This proverb is a warning to be careful what you say in front of children because they hear and understand, or misunderstand, more than you think: ♦ *Let's stop talking about Grandfather's illness; I hear the children coming and* ***little pitchers have big ears****.* ♦ *Now is not a good time to discuss what Christmas presents we are going to buy;* ***little pitchers have big ears*** *and we don't want to spoil the surprise.* ♦ *It must have been my daughter who told the other children about the surprise party, although I didn't think she heard me telling her father about it; still,* ***little pitchers have big ears****.*

Help

The proverb also has the forms **little pitchers have large ears** and **little pitchers have long ears**.

Did you know?

This proverb is a kind of play on words. A pitcher is an earthenware vessel having two ears or handles and used for carrying or storing water or other liquids.

Little strokes fell great oaks

Very large obstacles can be overcome by continuous and persistent effort: ♦ *Everyone said that the towns-people would never prevent the large factory being built in the fields behind the town. However, they organized a large protest group, gathered together a great deal of information from experts and eventually won, despite the power and money of the factory owners;* ***little strokes fell great oaks****.* ♦ *We thought that we had absolutely no chance of ever persuading the town council to build a new sports stadium. Still, after two years of hard campaigning, we eventually got their agreement;* ***little strokes fell great oaks****.*

Little things please little minds

People who are not very clever are easily pleased or amused. This is sometimes said about someone who seems to be getting an excessive amount of amusement out of something which is not very funny: ♦ *Janet laughed until she could hardly breathe when I lost my shoe in the sand;* ***little things please little minds****.* ♦ *George roared with laughter when Beth ran for the train and just missed it;* ***little things please little minds****.* ♦ *The neighbours seemed to think it was very amusing when someone parked a car across our driveway and prevented us from getting our car out;* ***little things please little minds****.*

Help

An alternative form of the proverb is **small things please small minds** and 'amuse' can be substituted for 'please' in both forms, as **little things amuse little minds**.

Live and let live

Similar

It takes all sorts to make a world.

This proverb advises you to show tolerance to others and allow them to live their lives in the way they want to, just as you wish to live yours the way you want to: ♦ *Janet always seems to be complaining about her neighbours' activities; I keep telling her to* ***live and let live****, but she pays no attention and continues to find them irritating.* ♦ *Jack says that he and Jenny don't see much of the other tenants in the block of flats, but it's a very amicable community; they all seem to adopt a policy of* ***live and let live****.* ♦ *Jenny doesn't really have anything in common with any of her flatmates, but they all seem to get on very well together; I think it's a case of* ***live and let live****.*

Look before you leap

Opposite

He who hesitates is lost.

You should think carefully about the possible consequences of something before you act. This proverb advocates caution and warns against rashness: ♦ *I know that you are in love with Martin and want to marry him right away, but you have only known him a few weeks. It is really best to* ***look before you leap****.* ♦ *I've been offered a new job with a very high salary in a new company which I don't know much about. I'm inclined to accept the offer, but my dad keeps telling me to* ***look before I leap****.* ♦ ***Look before you leap****; you might regret giving up your present flat to share with Mary and Anne and then you might not be able to get it back again.*

Lookers-on see more of the game

People who are not actually involved in something are more likely to have a true, or more objective, idea of what is going on: ♦ *Mike blamed Jane's behaviour for the break-up of their marriage and claimed that he had done nothing wrong. Yet it was quite obvious to everyone else that they had both behaved very badly;* ***lookers-on see more of the game****.* ♦ *Both countries were holding each other responsible for the start of the border skirmishes, each claiming that it was acting in self-defence. However, international observers were of the opinion that the war was the result of an old feud and both sides had to bear responsibility;* ***lookers-on see more of the game****.* ♦ *Bob's parents were convinced that he was being bullied at school, because he was always getting into fights. However, the teachers knew that he was the one who was doing the bullying;* ***lookers-on see more of the game****.*

Help

An alternative form of the proverb is **onlookers see more of the game** and 'most' can be substituted for 'more' in both forms.

Love is blind

People who are in love with someone are not aware of the faults of the person with whom they are in love: ♦ *Diane married Mark within a few weeks of meeting him and refused to believe what a dishonest person he is;* ***love is blind****.* ♦ ***Love is blind****; Beth's son is going out with a girl who quite clearly is only interested in his money, but he is the only one who does not appear to recognize this fact.* ♦ *Mike has had a long series of girlfriends and says that he has absolutely no intention of marrying her. Unfortunately, Lucy is convinced that he will change his mind and marry her;* ***love is blind****, as they say.*

Did you know?

This proverb may have its origin in the fact that Cupid, the Roman god of love, is sometimes represented in statues and paintings as being blindfolded.

Love makes the world go round

This proverb emphasizes the importance and power of love, indicating that the world could not operate without it: ♦ *It's good to see the young couple so much in love with each other; after all, it's* ***love that makes the world go round****.* ♦ *The head teacher is against having a school dance because she feels that it encourages romantic relationships between the students at a time when they should be concentrating on their studies and their exams. Cancelling the dance won't stop that; many of the young firmly believe that it's* ***love that makes the world go round****.* ♦ *Meg is a very romantic person who is convinced that* ***love makes the world go round****. However, she has a habit of falling in love with unromantic young men who seem to think that it is work which makes the world go round and work incredibly long hours.*

Love will find a way

This proverb emphasizes the power of love. When people are in love they seem to be able to overcome any obstacle which is put in the way of their love: ♦ *It's sad that June has been transferred to a branch of her firm overseas, while Mark has to stay here to finish his studies. Still, things will turn out all right if they really love each other;* ***love will find a way****.* ♦ *Harry has forbidden his daughter Julie to go on seeing Jimmy, because he thinks Jimmy is not good enough for her. Harry is being very foolish because if Julie is serious about Jimmy,* ***love will find a way****.* ♦ *Len and Olga met and fell in love at an international sports meeting, but have great difficulty in seeing each other, as she lives in Russia and he lives in Britain. Surely* ***love will find a way*** *and they will be together eventually.*

M

Make hay while the sun shines

You should take advantage of an advantageous situation or a good opportunity: ♦ *You should go out and enjoy yourself while you're waiting for your exam results. Very soon you'll have a full-time job and won't be able to;* ***make hay while the sun shines****.* ♦ *Estate agents are working very long hours just now, while the property market is booming; it's a case of* ***making hay while the sun shines****, especially when the boom is not expected to last much longer.* ♦ *The tourist season is quite a short one here and all the hotels and shops obviously try to make as much profit as possible; '****Make hay while the sun shines****' is their motto.*

Similar

Strike while the iron is hot.

Time and tide wait for no man.

Did you know?

The proverb has its origin in the uncertainty of the British climate. Farm workers had to work as hard and as long as possible on a fine day when the hay was being gathered in, because if rain came and prevented further work, the crop might be ruined.

Many a true word is spoken in jest

A joking or humorous remark may turn out to be a serious or true comment: ♦ *Harry was joking when he said that his wife was so extravagant that he would find himself bankrupt soon. It was a case of* ***many a true word spoken in jest****; soon after, Harry's business failed and he was, indeed, declared bankrupt.* ♦ ***Many a true word is spoken in jest****; Lucy was joking when she said that Jack must have something to hide, because he never spoke about himself. Jack had spent several years in prison and was, indeed, hiding the fact.* ♦ *On the way to the airport, Mary jokingly said that, since their taxi had been late and their train had been late, their plane would probably be late too.* ***Many a true word is spoken in jest*** *and their plane was delayed for three hours.*

Many hands make light work

Work does not take so long, and does not seem such a difficult task, if several people are involved in doing it: ♦ *We'll easily tidy up Granny's garden in an afternoon if we get all the family to help;* ***many hands make light work****.* ♦ *It shouldn't take long to clear up after the party if some of the guests volunteer to help;* ***many hands make light work****.* ♦ *We'd just moved house and had a great many boxes to unpack, but the neighbours kindly offered to help and it was amazing how quickly we got everything tidied away;* ***many hands make light work****.*

 *Similar*

Two heads are better than one.

Four eyes see more than two.

 *Opposite*

Too many cooks spoil the broth.

Marriage is a lottery

It is a matter of luck or chance whom you marry and whether you will be happy or not: ♦ *The bride and groom seem very much in love and let us hope that they will be very happy. Sadly, there is no certainty that they will be, because* ***marriage is a lottery****.* ♦ *Jill says that she is sure that she will one day meet the perfect man for her and live happily ever after. She refuses to believe that* ***marriage is a lottery****.* ♦ *Tom says that ten years ago he was at five weddings and now only two of the couples are still together, supporting his contention that* ***marriage is a lottery****.*

Opposite

Marriages are made in heaven.

Marriages are made in heaven

Marriage partners are arranged by God; therefore marriage should be a happy state: ♦ *It is impossible to believe that* ***marriages are made in heaven*** *when you look at Henry and his wife; how could God arrange a marriage that has made two people so unhappy?* ♦ *Pam has become engaged to Johnny and is going around saying that he is the perfect man for her and that* ***marriages are made in heaven****. God must have got it wrong the first time for Johnny because he is divorced.*

Opposite

Marriage is a lottery.

♦ *Sam's grandparents have been happily married for sixty years; seeing them together is enough to make one believe that* ***marriages are made in heaven****.*

Marry in haste and repent at leisure

If you rush into marriage too soon, you will have plenty of time to think about your mistake, and regret it, after the ceremony. This proverb is a warning not to marry someone whom you do not know very well: ♦ *Liz and Jack fell instantly in love when they met and married six weeks later, although it was obvious to both sets of family and friends that they were completely incompatible. It was a case of* ***marry in haste and repent at leisure*** *and they were both very unhappy until their divorce three years later.* ♦ *Mary told her parents that she wanted to marry Matt, whom she had just met and who had asked her to go to the other side of the world with him. They pleaded with her to wait until he returned from overseas, but she insisted and the wedding went ahead. It was a sad case of* ***marry in haste and repent at leisure*** *because Mary came home alone six months later, saying that the marriage was over.* ♦ *'****Marry in haste and repent at leisure****,' everyone told Clare and Tommy when they married a few weeks after their first meeting. Yet they have been very happy and celebrated their golden wedding last week.*

Might is right

One law for the rich and another for the poor.

Powerful people are often regarded as being right, simply because they are so powerful that less powerful people cannot challenge them successfully: ♦ *The largest, richest countries at the international conference are more likely to have their voices heard than the smaller ones;* ***might is right****.* ♦ *Sadly, I think Rob is right not to pursue his claim against the firm which sacked him. It's a huge multinational company and, as* *you know,* ***might is right****. ♦ The school has an advisory committee which has both student and teacher representatives, but the students complain that their views are rarely taken into consideration; it is a case of* ***might is right****.*

Misfortunes never come singly

Similar

It never rains but it pours.

Lightning never strikes twice in the same place.

If something bad happens to you, it's usual for other bad things to happen as well: ♦ *Jack's lost his job, his mother's in hospital and his car has just been stolen; he's certainly living proof that* ***misfortunes never come singly****.* ♦ ***Misfortunes never come singly****; yesterday I overslept, then I spilt coffee on my favourite white skirt and had to change it, then I got a scolding from the boss for being late and, finally, I got home to discover that the central heating system had broken down.* ♦ *Janet's car got a flat tyre on her way to work, which meant that she was late for an important appointment, and then she failed to secure a valuable order, which made her boss furious. It's true that* ***misfortunes never come singly****.*

Moderation in all things

This proverb warns us against doing or taking too much of anything: ♦ ***Moderation in all things****; having the occasional glass of wine will not do you any harm, but drinking a lot of spirits will damage your health.* ♦ *The doctor told James to take some light exercise after he recovered from heart surgery. But he spends hours at the gym every day and we are worried that he is over-doing it;* ***moderation in all things****.* ♦ *These exams are undeniably important and the students need to work hard, but they also need some leisure time;* ***moderation in all things****.*

Money is power

Those who have a lot of money usually also have a great deal of influence and power: ♦ *There is a suspicion that preference is given in the college to students with wealthy parents;* ***money is power****.* ♦ *Police have denied that charges have been dropped against the young man because he is the son of a wealthy businessman. But many people are of the opinion that* ***money is power*** *and don't believe the police.* ♦ ***Money is power*** *and the accused has enough money to appoint a very high-ranking barrister to defend him; he may well be found not guilty.*

Similar

Money talks.

Money is the root of all evil

Money is responsible for many of the crimes and acts of wrongdoing in the world: ♦ *There is a financial motive behind many murders;* ***money is the root of all evil****.* ♦ *The feud between the brothers began with a dispute over their father's will;* ***money is the root of all evil****.* ♦ *Mary and Bill are going through a very acrimonious divorce with a lot of argument over the division of their joint assets;* ***money is the root of all evil****.*

Did you know?

The proverb is a misquotation from the Bible. The original quotation is **the love of money is the root of all evil**, and it comes from 1 Timothy 6:10. The apostle Paul, writing to Timothy, says, 'For the love of money is the root of all evil, leading men to flounder in their Christian faith and fall into deep unhappiness.'

Money isn't everything

This proverb reminds us that we should not put too much value on money and material things; there are other important things in life: ♦ *Jim's parents are very ambitious for him and want him to have a well-paid career, but Jim says that* ***money isn't***

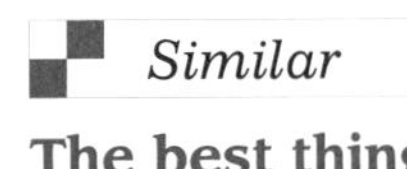

Similar

The best things in life are free.

Money is power.

Money talks.

everything *and wants to be an artist.* ♦ *I've been offered a highly paid job with a much larger firm, but I like my job here and I like my colleagues;* ***money isn't everything****.* ♦ *Jill and Brian both earn a great deal of money, but they work very long hours and never have any leisure time;* ***money isn't everything****.*

Money talks

■ *Similar*

Money is power.

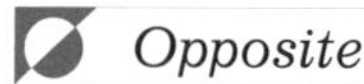

Money isn't everything.

The best things in life are free.

If you have wealth, you also have power and influence: ♦ *Most of the past presidents of the golf club have had a great deal of money;* ***money talks*** *when it comes to election time.* ♦ *Some of the poorer nations are challenging America's decision, but America is a very wealthy country and they are very unlikely to be successful;* ***money talks****.* ♦ *Most of the parents who are on the school board are wealthy businessmen or highly paid professionals;* ***money talks****.*

More haste, less speed

This is a warning that trying to do something in too much of a hurry can result in it taking longer to do than if you took more time and care; if you are in a hurry, you are apt to make careless mistakes: ♦ *I was making a cake in a great hurry and it was a case of* ***more haste, less speed****, because I forgot to put the eggs in and had to start again from scratch.* ♦ *You would be more likely to find your lost car key if you look for it calmly and carefully;* ***more haste, less speed****.* ♦ *Pam was packing her suitcase hurriedly just before she left for the airport. She kept forgetting what she had already put in the case and having to unpack it all again; it was a classic example of* ***more haste, less speed****.*

N

Necessity is the mother of invention

People will usually think of a way to cope with a difficult situation, often by using their imagination or ingenuity: ♦ *The baby was born very prematurely and the mother had no cot for it. But* ***necessity is the mother of invention****; we took one of the drawers out of the dressing table, and used it as crib.* ♦ *It was going to be several days before we could get the broken cottage windows repaired and so we cut up some cardboard boxes and used the cardboard to cover the inside of the windows;* ***necessity is the mother of invention****.* ♦ *The boots were too big for Pete, but he stuffed the toes with newspaper to try and make them fit better;* ***necessity is the mother of invention****.*

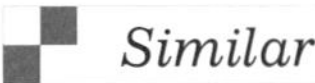

Needs must when the Devil drives.

Needs must when the Devil drives

Sometimes, because of circumstances, someone is forced to take a course of action which he or she does not want to take: ♦ *Jean didn't want to take a job in the factory, but she couldn't find any other employment and she had two children to feed;* ***needs must when the Devil drives****.* ♦ *They had absolutely no money left and Lucy had to sell her jewellery to pay for food;* ***needs must when the Devil drives****.* ♦ *The boss is sending Sue on a computer course at exactly the time she wanted to go on holiday and she cannot possibly refuse to go;* ***needs must when the Devil drives****.*

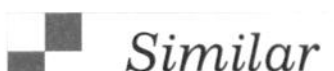

Necessity is the mother of invention.

Beggars can't be choosers.

Any port in a storm.

Help

The proverb above is a shortened form of **one needs must go when the Devil drives**.

Neither a borrower nor a lender be

This proverb warns against either borrowing or lending money: ♦ ***'Neither a borrower nor a lender***

Lend your money and lose your friend.

be' *is a proverb that is out of touch with modern life, because society today cannot operate without borrowing or lending.* ♦ *'**Neither a borrower nor a lender be**' was my grandfather's favourite proverb, which is funny, because several of his grandchildren have become bankers.* ♦ ***Neither a borrower nor a lender be**; I know that you feel sorry for Tom and want to lend him the money to pay his rent this month, but you don't have much money and if he can't pay you back you will get into debt yourself.*

Did you know?

The proverb has its origin in Shakespeare's play *Hamlet* and is a reference to some lines spoken by Polonius, father of Ophelia, to his son Laertes as the latter is about to set out on his travels:

Neither a borrower nor a lender be,
For loan oft loses both itself and friend,
*And borrowing dulls the edge of husbandry.**

*'Husbandry' here means the management of money.

Never is a long time

You should beware of saying that something will never happen, as unexpected things often happen: ♦ *People said that Aunt Jane would never marry, but **never is a long time** and she proved them all wrong by marrying when she was over 60.* ♦ *Ken always said that he would never sell the family business, but **never is a long time**. Now that he's old, with neither of his sons interested in taking over from him, he has sold it to one of his competitors.* ♦ *Jenny said that she was sure that she would never pass her driving test, having failed it three times. But **never is a long time**, and, after another set of lessons, she passed it easily.*

Never look a gift horse in the mouth

This proverb warns against being ungrateful and criticizing, or looking for faults in, something that you have received as a gift or obtained by chance: ♦ *Meg is so ungrateful she is complaining that the car her parents gave her as a birthday present is too small; someone should tell her* ***never to look a gift horse in the mouth****.* ♦ *Lisa's neighbour gave her a great many second-hand baby clothes which were in perfect condition, but Lisa criticized them for being old-fashioned; she should learn that it is best* ***never to look a gift horse in the mouth****.* ♦ ***Never look a gift horse in the mouth****; the rocking chair you bought at the car boot sale might not be in the best condition, but you can easily renovate it and you paid very little money for it.*

Did you know?

In origin, the proverb is a reference to the fact that people often gauge a horse's age by the state of its teeth.

Never put off till tomorrow what you can do today

This proverb urges us to deal with the things which we have to do right away rather than delay: ♦ *Mother frequently said '****Never put off till tomorrow what you can do today****' when we were growing up, but she herself never tackled anything right away.* ♦ *'****Never put off till tomorrow what you can do today****' is a sound piece of advice, but somehow it's easier to delay things than to follow the advice.* ♦ *Journalists never pay any heed to people who say, '****Never put off till tomorrow what you can do today****'; they never seem to be able to write anything until right before the deadline.*

Similar

Procrastination is the thief of time.

Delays are dangerous.

Tomorrow never comes.

Never trouble trouble until trouble troubles you

Don't anticipate trouble by worrying about something before it happens; it may never happen and

Similar

Don't cross the bridge till you come to it.

Don't cry before you are hurt.

Don't meet trouble halfway.

you will have worried unnecessarily: ♦ *There's no point in worrying what you will do if you fail your exams until you know for certain that you have failed;* ***never trouble trouble until trouble troubles you****.* ♦ *The doctor has just told you that you are quite well now, and you have no reason to suppose that your condition will get any worse;* ***never trouble trouble until trouble troubles you****.* ♦ *You may well not be one of those who are going to be declared redundant and so try not to be anxious;* ***never trouble trouble until trouble troubles you****.*

No man can serve two masters

You cannot be loyal to two people, organizations, systems or principles that are completely opposed to each other: ♦ *It is not surprising that John is having difficulty reconciling his left-wing political views with his executive position in business;* ***no man can serve two masters****.* ♦ ***No man can serve two masters*** *and yet Peter is a member of a church which is against materialism, while being a successful stockbroker in the city.* ♦ ***No man can serve two masters*** *and during the football World Cup, Mario had a real problem. He felt that he should be supporting England because he was born there, but his older relatives were all supporting Italy, where the family had come from.*

Did you know?

The proverb is biblical in origin, being an allusion to Matthew 6:24—'No man can serve two masters: for either he will hate the one, and love the other; or else he will hold to the one, and despise the other.' The two masters in this case are God and Mammon, the pagan god of wealth.

No news is good news

News about something unfortunate or unpleasant gets communicated from person to person very rapidly, and so if you have not heard anything about someone or something, nothing bad is likely to have taken place. The proverb is often used to calm those who are worrying: ♦ *You would have heard by now if Tom had been in an accident;* ***no news is good news*** *and I'm sure that he's perfectly all right.* ♦ *The hospital would have rung you if the blood tests you took last week were abnormal;* ***no news is good news****.* ♦ *I haven't heard from the garage and the mechanic said that he would ring if there was anything seriously wrong with the car;* ***no news is good news****.*

Similar
Bad news travels fast.

No pain, no gain

If you want to achieve something, you must be prepared to exert yourself or to put effort into it: ♦ *You're going to have to study hard if you want to pass your final exams;* ***no pain, no gain****.* ♦ *The team has a chance of winning the tournament, but they're going to have to train hard every day;* ***no pain, no gain****.* ♦ *If you want to get really fit, you're going to have to go to the gym regularly;* ***no pain, no gain,*** *as they say.*

Similar

Nothing venture, nothing gain.

No rose without a thorn

There is usually some flaw or disadvantage involved in some fortunate situation: ♦ *Bill seems the ideal candidate for the post, but he is said to have a very quick temper;* ***no rose without a thorn****.* ♦ *Jane will earn a lot of money in her new job, but she has to work some evenings and quite a few weekends;* ***no rose without a thorn****.* ♦ *The cottage is absolutely beautiful and just what we were looking for; it's a bit smaller than we would have liked, but* ***no rose without a thorn****.*

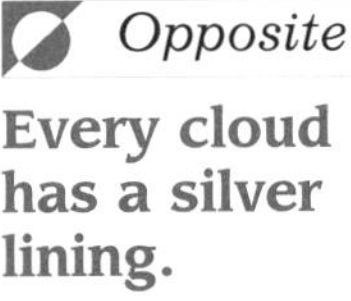
Opposite
Every cloud has a silver lining.

Nothing is certain but death and taxes

Similar

The unexpected always happens.

This proverb emphasizes the uncertain nature of most things in life: ♦ *It is usually very hot here in summer, but this year it's quite cold;* ***nothing is certain but death and taxes****, as they say.* ♦ *We were all sure that Pam would get the job because she was the best qualified candidate; still,* ***nothing is certain but death and taxes****.* ♦ *I was surprised when the taxi-driver failed to turn up to take me to the airport since he is usually very reliable and punctual; I suppose* ***nothing is certain but death and taxes****.*

Nothing succeeds like success

If you once succeed at something you are more likely to achieve further successes and to be held in high regard: ♦ *Winning the first round of the tournament would give Sara confidence and she might then go on to win the championship;* ***nothing succeeds like success****.* ♦ *Tom says that making a success of his first company was the difficult part. It was a case of* ***nothing succeeds like success*** *and the rest of his companies were profitable from the very start.* ♦ *The managing director was so impressed by Meg's presentation of the new product that he immediately offered her the job of marketing manager;* ***nothing succeeds like success****.*

Nothing venture, nothing gain

Similar

No pain, no gain.

If you never attempt anything or take any risks, you cannot be successful at anything: ♦ ***Nothing venture, nothing gain****; I think I'll enter the competition and see if I can win some prize money.* ♦ *I don't have all the qualifications listed in the ad for the job, but I'm going to apply for it, anyway,* ***nothing venture, nothing gain****.* ♦ *Tom likes Liz, but he doesn't think she will go out on a date with him. He should ask her anyway;* ***nothing venture, nothing gain****.*

Help

The proverb is also found in the alternative form **nothing ventured, nothing gained**.

O

Old habits die hard

It is difficult to stop doing something that you have been doing regularly for a long time: ♦ *Alex started to get ready for work this morning, forgetting that he had retired;* ***old habits die hard.*** ♦ *Liz still finds herself looking out of the window at five o'clock to see if her daughter's coming home from school. Her daughter left home last month to go to university, but* ***old habits die hard.*** ♦ *Bert still tries to put his foot on the clutch, even though his new car is an automatic one;* ***old habits die hard.***

Similar

You can't teach an old dog new tricks.

Opposite

You are never too old to learn.

Once bitten, twice shy

A person who has a bad experience concerning someone or something will not get involved with them in the future: ♦ *I promised myself I would never lend anyone any money again, because I gave Rob a loan last year and had great difficulty getting it back;* ***once bitten, twice shy.*** ♦ *Richard says that he would never use those builders again as the work they did on his house was substandard; it's a case of* ***once bitten, twice shy.*** ♦ *Lucy got her hair cut very badly at the local hairdresser's and vowed never to go there again;* ***once bitten, twice shy.***

Similar

A burnt child dreads the fire.

Did you know?

In origin, the proverb refers to someone avoiding a dog which has bitten them.

One good turn deserves another

Similar

You scratch my back and I'll scratch yours.

If someone does something to help someone else, then that person should, out of gratitude, do something to help the other person: ♦ *I'm late for work and my car won't start; I gave you a lift to the city last week and* ***one good turn deserves another****.* ♦ *I'm looking after my neighbour's dog while she's away for a few days; she always looks after my cat when I'm on holiday and* ***one good turn deserves another****.* ♦ *Jane often visits my elderly mother when I can't go and so I don't mind looking after her children sometimes;* ***one good turn deserves another****.*

One half of the world does not know how the other half lives

This proverb emphasizes the divide between the social classes, particularly the ignorance on the part of the rich of the kind of struggle which the poor experience: ♦ *When Meg was spending a holiday with her uncle who owned an estate, he took her to visit some of the cottagers and she was absolutely amazed and upset to see the poverty in which they lived;* ***one half of the world does not know how the other half lives****.* ♦ *Bob had always considered himself to be quite badly off until he became an aid worker for an international charity and visited parts of the world where abject poverty was the norm and famine was common. He then realized how true it is that* ***one half of the world does not know how the other half lives****.* ♦ *Sara always criticizes people who beg in the street and says that they are too lazy to find work. But as the proverb has it, '****One half of the world does not know how the other half lives****' and Sara is a very wealthy young woman who has no idea what it's like to be poor amd have no opportunity to improve.*

Help

The remark **how the other half lives!** is often used by someone with reference to the lifestyle of a person who is of a different social class from the person making the remark. It is used particularly of someone who has a more affluent lifestyle:

♦ *I had dinner with my boss and his wife last night and I couldn't believe the size of the house and the opulence of the place;* ***how the other half lives!***

One law for the rich and another for the poor

People without money and its accompanying influence and power are often treated more harshly than those who have money: ♦ *My neighbour's daughter was refused a place at that university and their lawyer's son, with exactly the same qualifications, was accepted; my neighbour is convinced that it was a case of* ***one law for the rich and another for the poor****.* ♦ *The local doctor was caught speeding by the police and got off with a warning. Yet one of our salesmen was fined heavily for the same offence and he wasn't driving nearly so fast as the doctor; it's* ***one law for the rich and another for the poor****.* ♦ *Anne is a very talented young tennis player, but her application for membership of the local club was rejected without an explanation. Her tennis coach is sure that it's a case of* ***one law for the rich and the another for the poor****; Anne's father is an unemployed labourer.*

Similar

Might is right.

One man's loss is another man's gain

There is usually someone who benefits from someone else's misfortune: ♦ *When Sam resigned from a rival firm last year, we offered him a job and we have found him to be an excellent worker;* ***one man's loss is another man's gain****.* ♦ *When Lucy had a row with the president of her tennis club, she resigned and we persuaded her to join ours. It's a case of* ***one man's***

Similar

It's an ill wind that blows nobody any good.

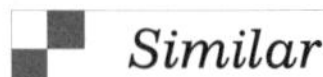

Every cloud has a silver lining.

loss is another man's gain *because she was their best player and is a real asset to our club.* ♦ *We paid less than the market value for the house because the sellers had to go abroad at short notice and required a quick sale;* ***one man's loss is another man's gain****.*

Help

The proverb often takes the form of sentences such as **his loss is our gain**:

♦ *Anna's competitors employed some of the workers whom she had to declare redundant when her fashion business was doing badly;* ***her loss was their gain****.*

One man's meat is another man's poison

Every man to his taste.

There is no accounting for tastes.

This proverb states that tastes differ and what one person likes another person might dislike very much: ♦ *Frank and his wife like old houses, but his daughter doesn't like them at all and wants to buy a brand-new one;* ***one man's meat is another man's poison****.* ♦ *Janet raved about the new play, but I thought it was extremely boring;* ***one man's meat is another man's poison****.* ♦ *The wedding dress had a great many frills and flounces and the bride loved it, although it was too fancy for my taste; still,* ***one man's meat is another man's poison****.*

Help

The proverb is sometimes shortened to **what's one man's meat**:

♦ *Bert says that Jane and Ron have decorated their house in the most ghastly colours, but* ***what's one man's meat****, as they say.*

Did you know?

The proverb has its origin in the work *De Rerum Natura* (45 BC), by Lucretius, a Roman poet and philosopher—'What's food to one may be fierce poison to another.'

One might as well be hanged for a sheep as a lamb

If you are going to be punished or criticized severely for something, it might as well be for a major offence, which will bring you more enjoyment, profit, etc, rather than a minor one: ♦ *It's already past the time I said I would be home and my parents are going to be very angry with me.* ***I might as well be hanged for a sheep as a lamb*** *and stay another couple of hours at the party.* ♦ *Liz said that she was already over her overdraft limit and that she was sure to get a nasty letter from the bank. Nevertheless, she bought yet more designer clothes, saying that* ***she might as well be hanged for a sheep as a lamb****.* ♦ *David said that if he was caught stealing a car he would be arrested; that being the case,* ***he might as well be hanged for a sheep as a lamb*** *and steal a large, expensive one.*

Similar

In for a penny, in for a pound.

Did you know?

In origin, the proverb refers to the fact that in England, the former penalty for stealing a sheep was death by hanging.

One picture is worth a thousand words

This proverb emphasizes the effectiveness of a picture in giving a description of something: ♦ ***A picture is worth a thousand words*** *and the newspaper photographs of the scene of the earthquake convey the sense of tragedy much more effectively than anything any journalist has written about it.* ♦ *I can't describe how happy Beth and Martin were on their wedding day, but here are the wedding photographs;* ***one picture is worth a thousand words****.* ♦ *You can see from the television coverage how terrible the plight of the famine victims is;* ***one picture is worth a thousand words****.*

One swallow does not make a summer

You should not assume that something, particularly something good, will happen on the basis of one single indication: ♦ *Certainly, Peter's present essay is much better than his previous work, but we must wait and see what his future essays are like before assuming that he has improved enough to go up to the next class;* ***one swallow does not make a summer***. ♦ *It would be over-optimistic to assume that sales will increase greatly this year on the basis of one month's improvement;* ***one swallow does not make a summer***. ♦ *The unemployment figures are down this month, but this could simply be a statistical blip. The government should remember that* ***one swallow does not make a summer***.

Did you know?

The proverb has its origin in an ancient Greek proverb which translates as 'One swallow does not make a spring.' In ancient Greece, the swallow was regarded as the herald of spring and there was much rejoicing when one was seen. One of Aesop's fables tells the tale of a young man, who, on seeing a swallow, assumed that spring had arrived and sold his winter coat to get money to spend on pleasure. Unfortunately for him, the swallow had mistaken a spell of unusually sunny weather for spring and had returned too early from its winter migration. When the cold weather returned, the young man regretted the sale of his coat, realizing that spring had not come after all.

Opportunity knocks but once

See **opportunity never knocks twice**.

Opportunity never knocks twice

Opposite

When one door shuts, another opens.

This proverb advises people to take advantage of an opportunity when it arises, as such an opportunity is not likely to occur again: ♦ *You would be a fool not to accept that offer of a job overseas; it may not be the best time for you to go, but* **opportunity never knocks twice**. ♦ *Houses in that area rarely come on the market and Jim is of the opinion that he and Anne should put in an offer for the one they saw, although it costs more than they can really afford; his attitude is that* **opportunity never knocks twice**. ♦ *We've been offered the free use of a friend's house in the south of France for a month and we've decided to accept the offer, even though it will be difficult for both of us to get off work for that length of time:* **opportunity never knocks twice**.

Help

The proverb sometimes appears in the longer form of **opportunity never knocks twice at any man's door**. An alternative form of the proverb is **opportunity seldom knocks twice** and a proverb with a very similar idea is **opportunity knocks but once**:

♦ *I would advise you to accept Joe's offer of an all-expenses-paid trip to America, even if it means postponing going to university until next year;* **opportunity knocks but once**.

Out of sight, out of mind

People often forget someone or something when they are not with them, however much they may claim to love them: ♦ *John and Sara fell wildly in love when they were on holiday in Spain. But at home they live miles from each other, and soon lost touch; it was a case of* **out of sight, out of mind**. ♦ *Tim treats his parents very well when he is living at home, but he rarely gets in touch with them when he is at university. It's a case of* **out of sight, out of mind**, *I suppose, and his parents get rather hurt.* ♦ *Pam absolutely adored her dogs when she was at home, but now that she is in a flat she never bothers about them, although her parents are too elderly to exercise them properly;* **out of sight, out of mind**, *unfortunately.*

 *Opposite*

Distance lends enchantment to the view.

Absence makes the heart grow fonder.

P

Patience is a virtue

This proverb urges us not to be impatient: ♦ *There's no point in getting agitated about not receiving a reply to your job application because you only sent it earlier this week;* ***patience is a virtue****.* ♦ *Their grandmother keeps telling the twins that* ***patience is a virtue****, but they pay no attention and are constantly asking if their birthday will soon be here.* ♦ *I know that it is Christmas morning and you want to open your presents, but it is a tradition in this house that presents are not opened until after the Christmas dinner; you'll just have to remember that* ***patience is a virtue****.*

Possession is nine points of the law

The person who actually has something is in the strongest position to keep it, if there is a dispute over ownership: ♦ *After Jim was installed in his hotel room, some people arrived claiming that they had booked that room in advance. Jim, however, declared that* ***possession is nine points of the law*** *and refused to move.* ♦ *Jill desperately wanted the blue sweater which was on offer at the boutique, but Sally got hold of it first;* ***possession is nine points of the law*** *and there was nothing Jill could do about it.*

Did you know?

This old proverb is not based on any specific law, but in early times people had to satisfy ten points (or, sometimes, twelve points) on some kind of scale in order to prove that they were entitled to something. An earlier alternative version of the proverb, now no longer used, **possession is eleven points of the law**, was based on the scale being made up of twelve points instead of ten.

Poverty is no disgrace

Being poor is nothing to be ashamed of, although many people look down on those who are poor: ♦ ***Poverty is no disgrace****; Jean's family are very poor and she is one of the cleverest and best-behaved students in the school.* ♦ ***Poverty is no disgrace****; the Brown family cannot help being poor because both parents are too ill to work.* ♦ *The other tenants in the block of flats look down on the Jacksons because they are so poor, but the parents are honest, hard-working people who have to clothe and feed their children on very low pay;* ***poverty is no disgrace****.*

Similar

Poverty is not a crime.

Help

This proverb is sometimes found in the longer form **poverty is no disgrace, but it is a great inconvenience**.

Poverty is not a crime

This proverb emphasizes the fact that people do not break the law just by being poor, although people often treat poor people as though they were wrongdoers; in fact, poverty can cause people to commit crime if they have not enough money to live on: ♦ *Mrs Jones is a terrible snob and is complaining bitterly that the people who have come to live across the road from her seem very poor; someone should tell her that* ***poverty is not a crime****.* ♦ ***Poverty is not a crime*** *and yet, whenever any petty burglary is committed, the police seem to think that the culprit is bound to be one of the many unemployed youths in the town.* ♦ *It is true that* ***poverty is not a crime****, but poverty has driven many a single mother to steal in order to feed her children.*

Similar

Poverty is no disgrace.

Help

An alternative form of this proverb is **poverty is no crime**.

Power corrupts

The acquisition of power seems to have a very bad effect on some people, making them dishonest or immoral, however honest they may have been before: ♦ *Before Mark was promoted to the post of office supervisor, he always seemed a very kind person. Last week, however, he refused to give one of the workers time off to take her daughter to the hospital;* ***power corrupts****, it seems.* ♦ *Before the politician was a member of the cabinet he was a very frank, honest person. But now he is regularly accused of giving false statements to the media and even of lying to parliament;* ***power corrupts****.* ♦ *It was hoped that after the coup, the new president would rule the country fairly. But, if anything, he is even more dishonest than the previous one;* ***power corrupts****.*

Help

The proverb is sometimes lengthened to **power corrupts and absolute power corrupts absolutely**, which is a reference to a statement in a letter by Lord Acton (1834–1902)—'Power tends to corrupt and absolute power corrupts absolutely.'

Practice makes perfect

In order to become very good at something, you have to practise doing it over and over again: ♦ *They say that* ***practice makes perfect****, but I think you need some talent as well. George has been practising golf strokes for years and he's still a hopeless player.* ♦ *Pam's mother believed implicitly that* ***practice makes perfect*** *and always insisted that Pam practised the piano every day after school; it put Pam off playing the piano for life.* ♦ ***Practice makes perfect****, and you will have to be prepared to spend a lot of time being coached if you want to become a professional tennis player.*

Prevention is better than cure

It is better to stop something happening than to be able to put it right or find a remedy for it afterwards: ♦ *Parents should be advised that if they stop their children from eating a lot of sweets, they will stop the spread of tooth decay;* ***prevention is better than cure****.* ♦ *Medical experts now believe that eating a diet which is rich in fruit and vegetables can reduce the incidence of heart disease;* ***prevention is better than cure****.* ♦ *We must make sure that all the factory workers are aware of the safety procedures which are in force, and that they follow them absolutely; there have been too many accidents recently and* ***prevention is better than cure****.*

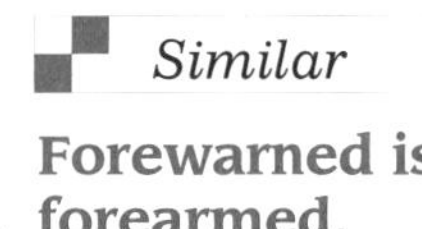

Similar

Forewarned is forearmed.

Pride goes before a fall

People who behave in a very vain or arrogant way often suffer some form of misfortune: ♦ *Bill was full of confidence before the exams, saying that he was sure to pass them easily, but he failed two of them;* ***pride goes before a fall****.* ♦ *Helen was always boasting about how well her daughter was doing at school, but then we heard that her daughter had been suspended for habitual truancy;* ***pride goes before a fall****.* ♦ *Lucy behaved very arrogantly to her former workmates after she got a job as publicity manager in another firm. But they've just discovered that her new firm is in financial difficulties and that she is likely to be declared redundant;* ***pride goes before a fall****, indeed.*

Similar

The bigger they are, the harder they fall.

Help

A modern alternative form is **pride comes before a fall**.

Did you know?

The proverb has a biblical origin. It is a reference to Proverbs 16:18—'Pride goeth before destruction, and an haughty spirit before a fall.' Earlier, archaic forms of it were **pride will have a fall** and **pride goeth before a fall**.

Procrastination is the thief of time

Never put off till tomorrow what you can do today.

Delays are dangerous.

Tomorrow never comes.

This is a warning against putting off doing things as delays waste time: ♦ ***Procrastination is the thief of time****; it is better to get your essay written today than to keep putting it off and spend time worrying about it.* ♦ *Sara's mother keeps telling her that* ***procrastination is the thief of time****, but Sara has rebelled against this and always puts everything off until the last possible minute.* ♦ *I keep telling myself that* ***procrastination is the thief of time****, but it doesn't make any difference; I still haven't finished decorating the room which I began to paint last year.*

Did you know?

The proverb has its origin in a line from a poem called 'Night Thoughts' (1742) by Edward Young—'**Procrastination is the thief of time**; Year after year it steals, till all are fled.'

Punctuality is the politeness of princes

Being punctual is an indication that you are well mannered and have been well brought up. This proverb is now considered formal: ♦ *Aunt May gets extremely angry when people are late; she says that* ***punctuality is the politeness of princes****.* ♦ *Old Mr Jones regrets that people never seem to be on time these days; he says that, when he was young, he was taught that* ***punctuality is the politeness of princes****.* ♦ *The youth nearly laughed out loud when he arrived late on the first day and his boss said, '****Punctuality is the politeness of princes****'; he had no idea what the man was talking about.*

Help

An alternative form of this proverb is **punctuality is the politeness of kings**.

R

Revenge is sweet

Taking revenge for a wrong which has been done to you is very satisfying: ♦ ***Revenge is sweet*** *and Tom took great pleasure in beating Roy in the final of the chess championship. The previous year Roy had won, but Tom was sure that he had cheated.* ♦ *The local golf club had turned down Matt's father's application and when it offered Matt membership, after he became local junior champion, he was happy to be able to decline;* ***revenge is sweet****.* ♦ *Mr and Mrs Smart had endured years of listening to loud music played by their neighbour's teenage children. When their grandson came to stay, after their neighbour's children had left home, they encouraged him to play music as loud as he liked;* ***revenge is sweet****.*

Similar

Hell hath no fury like a woman scorned.

Rome wasn't built in a day

This proverb advocates patience and perseverance by reminding us that it can take quite a lot of time to create or organize something important or worthwhile: ♦ *It will be a few days before the new production system is fully operational; changing over from the old system was a complicated task and* ***Rome wasn't built in a day****.* ♦ *Someone should tell Meg that* ***Rome wasn't built in a day****. This garden is a complete wilderness and she's expecting us to convert it into neat flowerbeds and immaculate lawns by the end of the week.* ♦ *Progress is definitely being made in the struggle against bullying in the school, but the new strategies have to be given time to take effect;* ***Rome wasn't built in a day****.*

Help

Ancient Rome was a city with many fine buildings and it would, obviously, have taken a considerable time to create.

S

Second thoughts are best

Look before you leap..

Opposite

He who hesitates is lost.

It is best to reconsider a decision before acting. This proverb is a warning against a hasty or impulsive action: ♦ *When I first heard what Jack had done, my reaction was to go round and shout at him. But I changed my mind and decided to ignore his action;* ***second thoughts are best****.* ♦ *Jill angrily handed in her resignation after her boss criticized her work. But when she calmed down, she gave the matter some more thought and asked if she could retain her job; fortunately, she realized that* ***second thoughts are best****.* ♦ *After her first major quarrel with John, Becky seriously thought about leaving him. Fortunately, she changed her mind and they've been quite happy ever since;* ***second thoughts are best****.*

Seeing is believing

When you actually see something, you can believe in its existence or believe that it is true: ♦ *I would not have believed that John had entered a church if I hadn't attended the same service as he did;* ***seeing is believing****.* ♦ *It seems incredible that the boy was able to climb through such a small gap, but I saw him do it and* ***seeing is believing****.* ♦ *When Bob described the size of the marrow which he grew, we were all extremely sceptical. Yet he was proved right when it was exhibited at the local horticultural show;* ***seeing is believing****.*

Seek and ye shall find

If you look hard enough for something you will find it; this advice is sometimes given humorously: ♦ *There are plenty of good jobs out there for people who are prepared to look for them; it is a case of* ***seek and ye shall find****.* ♦ *You're bound to find a university course which appeals to you, but you won't find it sitting and* *watching television;* ***seek and ye shall find****.* ♦ *Don't just sit there complaining about the fact that you haven't got a girlfriend when your college course is full of girls;* ***seek and ye shall find****.*

Did you know?

The proverb is biblical in origin, being a reference to Matthew 7:7—'Ask, and it shall be given you; seek, and ye shall find.'

Self-praise is no recommendation

There is no merit in praising yourself. This is a warning against boasting: ♦ *People are getting very tired of Paul telling everyone what a brilliant tennis player he is. Someone should tell him that* ***self-praise is no recommendation****.* ♦ *You may have played well, but it would be modest to wait for others to say so;* ***self-praise is no recommendation****.*

Set a thief to catch a thief

If you want to catch a wrongdoer, you should use the services of someone who has some experience of wrongdoing: ♦ *Fred was always very good at tax avoidance when he had his own business and now he's employed by the Inland Revenue; it's a case of* ***set a thief to catch a thief****.* ♦ *The local neighbourhood watch scheme has just appointed Tommy chairman. Although the others don't know this, it's a case of* ***set a thief to catch a thief****; Tommy served time in prison for burglary as a young man.* ♦ *The local council probably don't know that they've* ***set a thief to catch a thief****. They've just appointed Len to be a traffic warden; he has acquired quite a reputation for illegal parking and getting parking tickets over the years.*

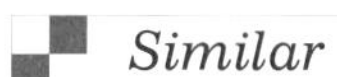
Similar

An old poacher makes the best gamekeeper.

Silence is golden

This proverb emphasizes the advantages or merits of silence or of not talking too much. It is sometimes used humorously: ♦ *I love the children dearly, but it is wonderful when they are all asleep;* ***silence is golden****.* ♦ *The shops and bars make a lot of money during the tourist season, but they appreciate the quietness when the tourists go;* ***silence is golden****, they find.* ♦ *I know why Pam left, but I'm not telling anyone.* ***Silence is golden*** *and I respect her wish to keep her reasons secret.*

Help

A longer form of this proverb is **speech is silver, but silence is golden**, which means that, although speech can be very useful, it is even more useful to know when not to say anything:

♦ *Our representative at the international conference could be very eloquent, but he decided that at this point, it would be better to make no comment. He made the right decision; it was one of those occasions when* ***speech is silver, but silence is golden****.*

Silence means consent

If you do not make any comment, it will be taken as a sign that you agree with, or accept, what has been said: ♦ *You should have denied the whole thing; now they will think you are guilty, as* ***silence means consent****.* ♦ *We assumed that Grace, as John's wife, would actively defend him when Jill criticized him. Instead, she said nothing and we are all aware that* ***silence means consent****.* ♦ *Beth queried the assumption that* ***silence meant consent****; she said that, although she disagreed vehemently with what he proposed, she was in such a state of shock that she could not say a word.*

Slow but sure wins the race

Patience and perseverance are likely to result in achievement and success. This is a warning that steady progress is better than rash haste when it comes to achieving things: ♦ ***Slow but sure wins the race****; since you haven't exercised for some time, you should start off with some light exercise and gradually work up to* *something more energetic.* ♦ *Harry was not a brilliant student, but he studied hard and regularly throughout the school year and he did extremely well in the exams;* ***slow but sure wins the race****.* ♦ *You will lose weight quickly on a crash diet, but it is bad for your health, and you will probably put weight on again when you stop it.* ***Slow but sure wins the race****; you should begin a healthy eating programme in which you will gradually lose weight.*

Help

The proverb is sometimes shortened to **slow but sure**, which, indeed, was the original form. A common variation of the proverb which has the same meaning is **slow and steady wins the race**:

♦ *It is much better to study on a regular basis throughout the year than to leave all your studying until just before the exam; it's a case of* ***slow and steady wins the race****.*

Did you know?

Both proverbs refer to Aesop's fable about the hare and the tortoise. The hare, being much faster than the tortoise, should have won the race easily. However, he was over-confident of winning, and after setting out at a fast pace and being very far in front of the tortoise, he sat down to have a rest and involuntarily fell asleep. The tortoise, moving at a very slow, but steady, pace, then passed the hare and won.

Something is better than nothing

This proverb advises us to be grateful for what we have or what we are given, even though it is not as much as we would like: ♦ *We really wanted a larger holiday apartment, but this was the only one left when we booked and we decided that* ***something was better than nothing****.* ♦ *Molly's grandfather left her a lot less money than she was hoping for, but it was enough to pay for an overseas holiday and* ***something was better than nothing****.* ♦ *The bank manger will lend Tom only a fraction of the money he wants for his new business, but Tom is philosophical about it and says that* ***something is better than nothing****.*

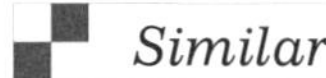

Half a loaf is better than no bread.

Enough is as good as a feast.

Sow the wind and reap the whirlwind

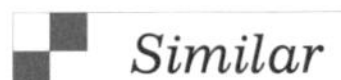

As you sow, so you reap.

As you make your bed, so you must lie on it.

If you do something bad, you will have to accept the even worse consequences which may follow: ♦ *A few soldiers started a border skirmish which eventually became a full-scale war between the two countries; they had **sowed the wind and reaped a whirlwind**.* ♦ *Molly stole the earrings from the shop because one of her school friends dared her to do it. She was caught, charged with shoplifting and fined; she had **sowed the wind and reaped the whirlwind**.* ♦ *When Jack challenged Len to a fight and beat him, he didn't know that Len was a member of a gang who would exact revenge on him; he **sowed the wind and is now reaping the whirlwind**.*

Help

An older, more formal version of the proverb is **they that sow the wind shall reap the whirlwind**.

Did you know?

The proverb is biblical in origin, being a reference to Hosea 8:7—'They have sown the wind, and shall reap the whirlwind.' This—and the previous proverb—is based on the idea of sowing seeds and gathering the crops which the seeds grow into.

Spare the rod and spoil the child

If you do not punish children when they have done wrong, they will become spoilt and badly behaved. Originally, this advice referred to corporal punishment, but is now applied more widely: ♦ *Diana's son has been sent to a child psychologist to try and find out what is causing him to behave so badly. But the child's grandfather thinks that Diana has been too lenient with the boy and that it is a case of **spare the rod and spoil the child**.* ♦ ***Spare the rod and spoil the child** was very much part of the Victorian attitude to children; many children received quite severe corporal punishment both at school and in* *the home.* ♦ *Mr Jones didn't mean it literally when he advised you not to* ***spare the rod and spoil the child****; he was merely suggesting that you rebuke your son, not beat him, for breaking the window.*

Help

The word 'rod' is a reference to the cane or stick which was used to administer corporal punishment.

Did you know?

The proverb is biblical in origin, being a reference to Proverbs 13:24—'He that spareth his rod, hateth his son.'

Speech is silver, but silence is golden

See **silence is golden**.

Still waters run deep

Quiet, calm people often have strong emotions and thoughts which they do not usually express and are often more complicated than they appear to be: ♦ *Tim was a very quiet person and never said a word when Jack teased him unmercifully, but one day he got up and hit Jack;* ***still waters run deep****, as they say.* ♦ *Everyone was surprised to learn that it was his wife who murdered Bill Jones because she was such a quiet, timid person. Alas,* ***still waters run deep*** *and she was, apparently, tired of being treated so badly by him.* ♦ *Bob usually has very talkative, outgoing girlfriends, but the girl who he is going to marry is very quiet and reserved. I hope* ***still waters run deep*** *or Bob is going to get bored with her.*

Help

It is often difficult to tell how deep and dangerous still or stagnant water is.

Strike while the iron is hot

Similar

Make hay while the sun shines.

Time and tide wait for no man.

Opposite

Look before you leap.

You should act immediately when an opportunity presents itself in order to achieve success: ♦ *The house comes on the market next week and you should* ***strike while the iron is hot*** *and put in an offer right away.* ♦ *There will never be a better time to buy shares in the company;* ***strike while the iron is hot****.* ♦ *Dad is in a very good mood at the start of his holiday and so now would be a good time to ask him for a loan;* ***strike while the iron is hot****.*

Did you know?

The proverb has its origin in the fact that blacksmiths did not hammer the metal they were using until it was extremely hot.

Sufficient unto the day is the evil thereof

Similar

Never trouble trouble until trouble troubles you.

Concentrate on today's problems and do not worry about those which might happen in the future: ♦ *For the moment you have a job, and there is no point in worrying about what might happen next year;* ***sufficient unto the day is the evil thereof****.* ♦ *We don't yet know if the landlord will renew the lease of our flat, but the lease is not due to be renewed until the end of the year;* ***sufficient unto the day is the evil thereof****.* ♦ ***Sufficient unto the day is the evil thereof****; it's foolish to worry about what you'll do when your present contract has come to an end, because it has another year to run and anything can happen in a year.*

Help

The proverb is often shortened to **sufficient unto the day** and is more widely used than the formality of its wording suggests.

Did you know?

The proverb has a biblical origin, being a reference to Matthew 6:34. At the end of his Sermon on the Mount, Jesus said, 'Take, therefore, no thought for the morrow; for the morrow shall take thought for the things of itself. Sufficient unto the day is the evil thereof.'

T

Take care of the pence and the pounds will take care of themselves

If you are careful about how you manage small amounts of money, you do not have to worry about how to manage large amounts: ♦ *All his life Henry has been of the opinion that if you* ***take care of the pence, the pounds will take care of themselves****. Even as a child he was very thrifty and saved most of his pocket money.* ♦ *George is now a billionaire and claims that he amassed his great wealth because he had followed his father's advice from an early age—'****Take care of the pence and the pounds will take care of themselves****.'* ♦ *'****Take care of the pence and the pounds will take care of themselves****' was our grandfather's favourite saying. Unfortunately, none of us paid any attention and always spent all we earned; now we are all broke.*

Help

An alternative form of this proverb is **look after the pence and the pounds will look after themselves**, and 'pennies' can be substituted for 'pence' in both forms.

Did you know?

The proverb has been ascribed to William Lowndes (1652–74), who was Secretary of the Treasury and known for his thrift.

Talk of the Devil, and he will appear

This is said when a person who was being talked about suddenly appears: ♦ ***Talk of the Devil, and he will appear****; we were just saying that it's a long time since we saw you and now here you are.* ♦ ***Talk of the Devil, and he will appear****; Joan was just telling Mary that she thought Bill had left town, when he walked into the room.* ♦ *We were just having a drink and discussing* *the good times we'd had with Lucy before she went away to college, when she came into the bar and waved at us:* ***talk of the Devil, and he will appear****.*

Help

The proverb has the alternative form **talk of the Devil, and he is bound to appear**, and 'speak' can be substituted for 'talk' in both forms, as **speak of the Devil, and he will appear**. The proverb is often shortened to **talk of the Devil**:

♦ ***Talk of the Devil****; I was just mentioning that I hadn't seen George for ages and there he is!*

The apple never falls far from the tree

Similar

Blood will tell.

What's bred in the bone will come out in the flesh.

A child tends to be close in character to a parent. This proverb is often used to suggest that someone has inherited the bad character traits of one of his or her parents: ♦ *Although Jack seems very honest, remember that his father is an utter rogue and that* ***the apple never falls far from the tree****.* ♦ *Bob says that his girlfriend is nothing like her bad-tempered, nagging mother, but we've all seen her in a very bad mood and* ***the apple never falls far from the tree****.* ♦ *I wouldn't believe everything Amy says; all her family are very deceitful and* ***the apple never falls far from the tree****.*

The bad workman blames his tools

People often blame their own incompetence or lack of success on something, such as their equipment, when in fact they themselves are to blame: ♦ *Sue said that the computer wasn't working properly, but the problem was that she didn't know how to use it;* ***the bad workman blames his tools****.* ♦ *Fred said that there must have been something wrong with the plants which he bought, because they all died when he planted them in his garden, but he had forgotten to water them;* ***the bad workman blames his tools****.* ♦ *Jill says that her cakes never turn out very well because she doesn't have a very accurate oven, but it's a case of* ***a bad workman blaming his tools****.*

The best of friends must part

However close or dear friends are to each other, there is always a point in their lives when, because of circumstances, they have to experience a period of separation, whether temporary or permanent: ♦ *Meg and I were very close friends throughout our time at university, but when we graduated I went to work in London and she went overseas; we missed each other, but* ***the best of friends must part****.* ♦ *It is difficult for children to appreciate that* ***the best of friends must part****; Jill and Mary have been best friends all through primary school, but now they are going to different secondary schools and they are very upset.* ♦ *We are really sad that our next-door neighbours are moving house to another part of the country; we have become really good friends with them, but I suppose it's true that* ***the best of friends must part****.*

All good things must come to an end.

The best things come in small packages

Things of good quality often come in small amounts: ♦ *Jim brought me a tiny bottle of perfume back from France, but it smelt wonderful and was very expensive;* ***the best things come in small packages****.* ♦ *The small packet in the fridge contains truffles;* ***the best things come in small packages*** *and they are a real delicacy, if rather expensive.*

Help

The proverb can also be applied to people, especially when used in humorous contexts:

♦ *Mary's husband is not a lot smaller than she is; but she says that the* ***best things come in small packages****.*

A common humorous reply to the proverb is, 'So does poison.' The proverb can also take the form of **the best things come in small parcels**; **good things come in small packages** and **good things come in small parcels**.

The best things in life are free

Similar

Money isn't everything.

Opposite

Money is power.

Money talks.

Those things in life which add most to the quality of life, and which are most enjoyable and worthwhile, do not cost any money: ♦ *We went for a lovely walk in the country; the air was fresh, the sun was shining and all the spring wild flowers were blooming, reminding us that* ***the best things in life are free***. ♦ *Their parents don't have enough money to take the children on holiday or to go on any excursions with them, but there are a great many things for them to do that don't cost money;* ***the best things in life are free*** *and they can play with their friends in the back garden, go for walks in the park, feed the ducks on the pond, or picnic by the river.* ♦ *Jack said that after he had had a major health scare and nearly died, he realized how true it was that* ***the best things in life are free***. *He suddenly appreciated the leaves on the trees, the flowers in the garden and children laughing in a way which he had not done before.*

Did you know?

The saying features in a song by American songwriters Buddy de Sylva (1895–1950) and Lew Brown (1893–1958):

The moon belongs to everyone,
The best things in life are free.
The stars belong to everyone,
They gleam there for you and me.

The bigger they are, the harder they fall

Similar

Pride goes before a fall.

The more important you are, the greater will be your failure if things go wrong, because you have a great deal to lose: ♦ *Pete's brother is very arrogant now that he is a successful businessman, but a great many businesses like his are facing money difficulties just now; it might be a case of* ***the bigger they are, the harder they fall***. ♦ *Our local councillor was becoming quite well known in national politics until the newspapers published* *a story about some fraudulent financial scheme in which he had been involved, and that was the end of his political career and his business career;* ***the bigger they are, the harder they fall.*** ♦ ***The bigger they are, the harder they fall****; Jane was always boasting about her father being the chief executive of a multinational, but he has just been made redundant.*

Help

An alternative form is **the bigger they come, the harder they fall**.

Did you know?

The origin of this saying is often attributed to boxer Robert Fitzsimmons. Just before one of his fights, which took place around 1900, he is said to have commented, 'If I can get close enough, I'll guarantee to stop almost anybody. The bigger the man, the heavier the fall.' However, the sentiment of the saying is found in *Proverbs* hundreds of years before this.

The darkest hour is just before the dawn

Things always seem at their worst just before they begin to improve. This proverb is often used to give hope to someone who is experiencing a time of trouble or difficulty: ♦ *No wonder you're feeling depressed just now because you've just lost your job, but* ***the darkest hour is just before the dawn****, and you'll probably get a reply to some of your job applications very soon.* ♦ *Tom is quite ill just now, but his doctors hope that he will improve once the medication begins to take effect;* ***the darkest hour is just before the dawn****.* ♦ *Pam is feeling very low because her husband has just left her, leaving her with very little money to keep herself and the children. Although I've tried telling her* ***the darkest hour is just before the dawn*** *and that things are bound to improve soon, I know that she doesn't really believe it.*

Similar

After a storm comes a calm.

The Devil finds work for idle hands to do

Those who are not kept busy by work or some other useful activity will start doing things which are bad, harmful or mischievous: ♦ *The youths are unemployed and seem to spend their time vandalizing other people's property;* ***the Devil finds work for idle hands to do****.* ♦ *It's important to keep the children occupied during the long summer holidays so that they have no time to get up to mischief;* ***the Devil finds work for idle hands to do****.* ♦ *The fire was started by children who were bored and started playing with a box of matches;* ***the Devil finds work for idle hands to do****.*

The early bird catches the worm

Similar

First come, first served.

The sooner begun, the sooner done.

You should act promptly and punctually if you want to achieve something: ♦ *If you want to be certain of getting tickets for the pop concert, you will have to be at the box office as soon as it opens. The concert will be very popular and* ***the early bird catches the worm****.* ♦ *Sally was very keen to get a part in the play, but she didn't reach the theatre until the auditions were over. She's always late and needs someone to remind her that* ***the early bird catches the worm****.* ♦ *I bought the local newspaper as soon as the shop opened this morning and phoned up about the flat that was advertised right away; it was a case of* ***the early bird catches the worm*** *and I move into the flat next week.*

Help

The phrase **the early bird** is often used to refer to someone who acts promptly or someone who gets up early in the morning:

♦ *Jim was the first person to apply for the new course; he's always* ***an early bird****.* ♦ *Jill's* ***an early bird*** *this morning; she had breakfast with me and she doesn't usually get up until long after I've gone to work.*

The end justifies the means

If the result of an action is good, it does not matter if the action which achieves this result is morally wrong, unjust, violent, etc. This proverb is sometimes used to try to justify an action which is not really excusable: ♦ *The police may not have told the truth when they got the murderer to confess, but the man was proved in court to be a dangerous killer;* ***the end justifies the means****.* ♦ *It may have seemed cruel of Lisa to tell Alice that her fiancé was going out with someone else, but surely it was better for her to find out what he was like before she married him;* ***the end justifies the means****.* ♦ *When he persuaded his grandmother to see a doctor, Dan did not tell the old lady that the doctor had told him that he would almost certainly have to admit her to hospital for tests and she was very angry. The old lady would not have kept the appointment if she had known;* ***the end justifies the means****.*

The exception proves the rule

The fact that an exception has to be made for something because it is not in accordance with a particular rule, law or belief proves the existence of a general rule, law or belief. This proverb is now often used to try to justify something which is inconsistent or contradictory: ♦ *Jackie was always saying that all attractive men are vain, but her latest boyfriend is very attractive and she says that* ***the exception proves the rule*** *because he is quite modest.* ♦ *Fred has long been of the opinion that all small country towns are boring, but he spent the summer in one for work reasons and liked living there very much; he says that* ***the exception proves the rule****.* ♦ *As a rule, houses in that area are modern and rather ugly, but this one is* ***the exception which proves the rule****; it is quite old, beautifully proportioned and very elegant.*

Help

The proverb is a shortened form of a legal phrase: **the exception proves the rule in cases not excepted**.

The eyes are the window of the soul

You can tell a lot about a person's character from looking at his or her eyes and the expression there: ♦ *Alice was very hospitable to us when we arrived unexpectedly, but she had a very hard expression in her eyes and* ***the eyes are the window of the soul****.* ♦ *Sam says that* ***the eyes are the window of the soul*** *and that people can tell that Jill's really honest just by looking at her wide open eyes.* ♦ *Pete pretends to be a very open, frank person, but his eyes always seem to have a very sly expression and* ***the eyes are the window of the soul****.*

Help

Another version of this proverb is **the eyes are the windows of the heart**.

The good die young

This proverb suggests that virtuous people die at a younger age than others do; it is often used now in humorous contexts: ♦ *Mrs Morton said it was a case of only* ***the good die young*** *when her youngest son died just before his fourteenth birthday. If he had lived, he might have become an unruly teenager like her other sons.* ♦ *Old Jimmy seems to be quite ill, but if it's true that* ***the good die young****, he'll be with us for quite some time; he smokes, drinks too much and has been in prison several times.* ♦ *Joan is a real hypochondriac. Every time she has a minor cold, she decides that it is something fatal and starts planning her own funeral; we keep telling her that only* ***the good die young****, but it makes no difference.*

The grass is always greener on the other side of the fence

Life always seems better somewhere other than where you are living or working, or someone else's situation always seems better than yours. This proverb is often used to suggest that people should be content with their present situation: ♦ *Alice and Tom have moved house four times in three years because Alice is never satisfied with a house once she's in it and always thinks another area of town will be preferable. It's a classic case of* ***the grass is always greener on the other side of the fence****.* ♦ *Jack was always complaining and looking for other jobs when he worked with us, but when he moved to another firm he behaved in the same way. For Jack,* ***the grass is always greener on the other side of the fence*** *and I doubt if he will ever find work satisfaction anywhere.*

Help

This proverb is often shortened to **the grass is always greener**:

♦ *As soon as Anna has been going out with someone for a few weeks, she gets bored with him, starts looking around for a new boyfriend and then the whole process begins again; as far as Anna is concerned,* ***the grass is always greener****.*

The proverb is so widely used that it has become a cliché, especially in its shortened form.

The labourer is worthy of his hire

People deserve to be paid for the work that they do: ♦ *Sam said that he would be happy to help Lucy with her maths, provided her parents paid him. This was fair enough,* ***as the labourer is worthy of his hire****.* ♦ *The president of the club is a friend of a friend of mine and he asked me if I would have a look at their accounts as a favour to him. Unfortunately, I have a great deal of work at the moment and, in any case, it is my belief that* ***the labourer is worthy of his hire****; I don't work for nothing.* ♦ *The pastor asked for volunteers to do*

Miss Brown's gardening work, as it was now too much for her. One of the boys pointed out that, unlike some of the old people in the community, Miss Brown could well afford to pay a gardener; ***the labourer is worthy of his hire****.*

The leopard does not change his spots

The basic characteristics, usually undesirable ones, of a person do not change: ♦ *Jane hopes that Mike will lose his love of travel when they marry and settle down, but* ***the leopard does not change his spots****.* ♦ *When Lily, who is noted for her unpunctuality, first started going out with Ken, she amazed us all by arriving on time everywhere. But she soon started being late again;* ***the leopard does not change his spots****.* ♦ *After Ron had been reprimanded severely by the head teacher, he began to attend lessons regularly and his teachers were very pleased. However, in a short space of time he began to play truant again;* ***the leopard does not change his spots****.*

Help

This proverb sometimes appears in the form **the leopard cannot change his spots** and 'its' is sometimes substituted for 'his' in both forms. The idiomatic phrase **change his (its) spots** is also quite common:

♦ *Amazingly, Billy seems to have* ***changed his spots*** *since he got married. He used to be a wild character who went out with his friends every night, but now he spends every evening at home.*

Did you know?

The origin of the proverb lies in the Old Testament of the Bible. Referring to the fact that sin seemed to have become ingrained in his people, the prophet Jeremiah asks, 'Can the Ethiopian change his colour or the leopard his spots?' (Jeremiah 13:23).

The more the merrier

The more people who are involved in something the more enjoyable or more successful the occasion will be: ♦ *We are having the picnic in a large field and there are no restrictions on the number of children who can take part;* ***the more the merrier****.* ♦ *The art exhibition is free and open to everyone;* ***the more the merrier****.* ♦ *The minister welcomes everyone to his church, not just members of the congregation;* ***the more the merrier****.*

 *Opposite*

Too many cooks spoil the broth.

The more you get, the more you want

People are greedy and are never satisfied with what they have: ♦ *Young couples seem to work very hard these days to earn a lot of money to buy more and more possessions;* ***the more you get, the more you want****.* ♦ *The workers got a very large bonus last year and they are expecting an even larger one this year, although the company has not been doing so well;* ***the more you get, the more you want****.* ♦ *The children already have a huge number of toys, but, whenever a toy is advertised on television, they ask for it;* ***the more you get, the more you want****.*

 *Opposite*

Enough is as good as a feast.

The pen is mightier than the sword

Words are more effective than weapons; the implication is that people should write or talk to each other to try to settle their differences, instead of going to war or having a physical fight: ♦ *It is important that we try to convince the two nations that* ***the pen is mightier than the sword*** *and keep them communicating with each other; otherwise, there is a very real danger of war.* ♦ ***The pen is mightier than the sword****; apparently, one of John's ancestors challenged one of mine to a duel, but this was avoided by an exchange of letters which brought the quarrel to an end.* ♦ *Paul wanted to challenge Daniel to a fight, because Daniel had been seen at a party with Paul's girlfriend* *while Paul was working in another town. Mike persuaded Paul that* ***the pen was mightier than the sword*** *and Paul wrote to Daniel asking for an explanation; Daniel was able to explain that the whole thing was a misunderstanding.*

Did you know?

The idea behind this proverb is a very old one, but the actual wording of it has been ascribed to Edward George Bulwer-Lytton, who wrote in his play *Richelieu* (1839): 'Beneath the rule of men entirely great, / The pen is mightier than the sword.'

The proof of the pudding is in the eating

How successful something is will be established only when it has been used or put into practice: ♦ *We won't know how efficient the new filing system is until we have actually started using it;* ***the proof of the pudding is in the eating.*** ♦ ***The proof of the pudding is in the eating;*** *the traffic proposals for the town centre look fine on paper, but we won't know if they will reduce congestion until they are put into practice.* ♦ *The head teacher has proposed some new guidelines for dealing with truancy, but we won't know how effective they are until they have been in force for a few weeks;* ***the proof of the pudding is in the eating.***

Help

The noun 'proof' in this sense means to test. Thus, literally, how successful the pudding is will not be known until it has been tested by someone eating it.

The road to hell is paved with good intentions

People can have extremely good intentions and still act wrongly or inappropriately: ♦ *The social workers thought that they were doing the right thing in taking the child away from the mother. Still, it turned out that she was an extremely caring mother and soon got her child back;* **the road to hell is paved with good intentions**. ♦ *Mike thought that he was being helpful by letting the boy stay at his flat. But apparently the police were looking for the youth and Mike had unwittingly helped him to escape from them;* **the road to hell is paved with good intentions**. ♦ *Rose's new next-door neighbour is disabled and Rose has been offering to do his shopping and help him in various ways. But, apparently he is fiercely independent and thinks that Rose is patronizing him;* **the road to hell is paved with good intentions**.

Help

An alternative form of the proverb is **the way to hell is paved with good intentions**.

The sooner begun, the sooner done

The sooner you start something, the sooner you will finish it. This proverb advises against delaying things: ♦ *You should do your homework this evening and then you will have the rest of the weekend free;* **the sooner begun, the sooner done**. ♦ *I don't really want to dig the garden this weekend, but I suppose I'd better get on with it;* **the sooner begun, the sooner done**. ♦ *It won't take you long to deal with your correspondence and then you can stop worrying about it;* **the sooner begun, the sooner done**.

Similar

Never put off till tomorrow what you can do today.

Well begun is half done.

The early bird catches the worm.

The unexpected always happens

However much we plan, things which we could not have foreseen or expected always happen: ♦ *We had planned our holiday to the last detail, but* **the unexpected always happens**. *In this case, it was a strike of baggage handlers at the local airport.* ♦ *Everyone thought that last year's champion would win this year's tournament easily, but he was beaten in the second round by a young, unknown player;* **the unexpected always**

Similar

Nothing is certain but death and taxes.

happens. ♦ *We have been coming here on holiday for years and the weather has always been dry and sunny, but this year there has been heavy rain and flooding;* ***the unexpected always happens****.*

The way to a man's heart is through his stomach

The way to get a man to like you is to prepare good things for him to eat. This proverb is often used humorously: ♦ *Pam says that* ***the way to a man's heart is through his stomach*** *and so she has decided to invite her new boyfriend to dinner to show off her cooking skills.* ♦ *If* ***the way to a man's heart is through his stomach****, then Sara is not likely to get married; she can't even make toast without burning it.* ♦ *Jane says that she is going to cookery classes because she likes good food, and not because* ***the way to a man's heart is through his stomach****. Yet she makes no secret of the fact that she is looking for a husband.*

There are as good fish in the sea as ever came out of it

This proverb is often used to indicate that there are plenty of opportunities still available, although some may have been lost. This proverb is often used of potential husbands, wives or partners as a way of comforting someone who has lost a partner: ♦ *Mark doesn't seem very worried about losing his job. I think he's taking the attitude that* ***there are as good fish in the sea as ever came out of it*** *and he is very well qualified.* ♦ *Tony is feeling very miserable because Liz has gonc off with someone else, but he'll soon realize that* ***there are as good fish in the sea as ever came out of it****.*

Help

A modern and shorter version of this proverb is **there are plenty more fish in the sea**:

♦ *Diana is sitting at home, feeling sad about Terry leaving her and refusing to listen to us when we tell her that* ***there are plenty more fish in the sea****.*

There are more ways of killing a cat than choking it with cream

There are several possible ways of achieving the same result or aim: ♦ *You didn't have to be so rude to Grace to let her know that you weren't interested in her;* ***there are more ways of killing a cat than choking it with cream****.* ♦ *Peter says that he is reluctant to tell his tenants bluntly to move out, but he wants them to go and he will, undoubtedly, find a more subtle method;* ***there are more ways of killing a cat than choking it with cream****.* ♦ *Jim is not so foolish as to get his revenge on Mike by challenging him to a fight, but he will get his own back somehow;* ***there are more ways of killing a cat than choking it with cream****.*

Similar

There is more than one way to skin a cat.

Help

The proverb has the same meaning as **there is more than one way to skin a cat**.

Did you know?

The proverb has its origin in the novel *Westward Ho* (1855) by Charles Kingsley.

There are two sides to every question

There are two differing points of view in every dispute, proposal, etc: ♦ *Helen was telling everyone that it was Jack's unacceptable behaviour which led them to break up. Still,* ***there are two sides to every question****, and most people say that Helen did not behave very well either.* ♦ *Mike is very much in favour of the proposal to* *expand the company, but he has not considered any of the disadvantages and* ***there are two sides to every question****.* ♦ *Janet said that her brother was entirely responsible for the fact that she and he are estranged. However, we haven't heard the brother's point of view and* ***there are two sides to every question****.*

Help

The Greek philosopher Protagoras is credited with first putting forward the idea behind this proverb.

There is a time and a place for everything

Similar

There is a time for everything.

This proverb emphasizes the importance of appropriateness and suitability. It is often said to suggest that someone's action is not appropriate or proper in the circumstances: ♦ *George's action in asking to see his grandmother's will immediately after the funeral was in appallingly bad taste;* ***there is a time and a place for everything****.* ♦ *I have no objection to the neighbour's teenage children listening to music, so long as they don't do it after midnight in the bedroom adjoining mine;* ***there is a time and a place for everything****.* ♦ *Please don't mend your bicycle in the kitchen when I am trying to cook dinner;* ***there is a time and a place for everything*** *and the best place to do that is the garage.*

Help

The proverb is sometimes shortened to **there's a time and a place**:

♦ *Please do not practise the violin in your bedroom at night;* ***there's a time and a place****.*

There is a time for everything

Everything has its appointed time. This proverb emphasizes the importance of doing things at an appropriate and fitting time: ♦ ***There is a time for***

everything *and the time for doing your homework is not at breakfast time when the work should be ready for handing in.* ♦ *I don't mind the children watching television, but not at this time of night when they should be in bed;* ***there is a time for everything.*** ♦ *You shouldn't be studying so late;* ***there is a time for everything*** *and right now you need to get some sleep.*

Similar

There is a time and a place for everything.

Did you know?

The proverb has a biblical origin, being a reference to Ecclesiastes 3:1—'To everything there is a season, and a time to every purpose under the heaven.'

There is always a first time

Just because something, particularly something bad, has not happened so far, it does not mean that it will never happen: ♦ *Jack always drives so fast and boasts that he has never been stopped by the police. But* ***there's always a first time*** *and, if he loses his driving licence, he will lose his job.* ♦ *Jill has been lucky so far in that the boss hasn't caught her arriving at work late, but* ***there's always a first time*** *and he has strict rules about punctuality.* ♦ *Beth leaves her car there every day and so far has not got a parking ticket, but* ***there's always a first time*** *and there are now more parking wardens operating in the area.*

Help

An alternative form of the proverb is **there is a first time for everything**.

There is honour among thieves

Thieves and other wrongdoers may cheat, deceive and steal from others, but they do not treat each other in this way: ♦ *When he was arrested, the pickpocket said that he did not usually operate in that area, as it was his cousin's territory;* ***there is honour among thieves.*** ♦ *The market trader conned an old lady out of a lot of money when he bought a valuable vase* *from her for a pittance. He himself was also going to sell it for much less than it was worth, until a fellow trader, who was in the same line of business as himself, advised him on the right price to ask;* ***there is honour among thieves****.* ♦ *The two taxi drivers made a fortune in the tourist season by overcharging visitors, but they didn't try to cheat each other and scrupulously divided all the profits at the end of each day;* ***there is honour among thieves****.*

There is more than one way to skin a cat

There is more than one way to achieve a result or aim: ♦ *You could work during the day and go to evening classes and still get the same qualification as you would from a full-time university course;* ***there is more than one way to skin a cat****.* ♦ ***There is more than one way to skin a cat****; if Ruth won't accept rent from you for living in her spare room, you could help her with her child-care problems.* ♦ *The bank may have refused Bert a loan to start his publishing business, but he's determined to go ahead; he says that* ***there is more than one way to skin a cat****.*

Help

This proverb has the same meaning as **there are more ways of killing a cat than choking it with cream**.

There is no accounting for tastes

Similar

One man's meat is another man's poison.

It is impossible to explain why some people like some things and others like quite different things. The proverb is often used to refer to tastes which are not in agreement with our own: ♦ *Jane was invited to join some friends who have rented a villa in southern France, but she has decided to spend her holiday climbing hills in a very wet part of the country;* ***there's no accounting for tastes****.* ♦ *Molly made a wonderful chocolate mousse for dessert, but some of the children* *said that they preferred the one made out of a packet which they usually had at home;* ***there's no accounting for tastes****.* ♦ ***There's no accounting for tastes****; Harry actually likes that ghastly wallpaper.*

Every man to his taste.

There is no smoke without fire

Rumours often have an element of truth in them; otherwise the rumour would not have started in the first place: ♦ *I've heard from various people that Dick was sacked for embezzling money from the firm and* ***there is no smoke without fire****.* ♦ *It seems very unlikely that John is a police suspect for the murder of his brother, but the story is all over the town and* ***there is no smoke without fire****.* ♦ *The rumours about Jill being arrested for shoplifting are completely untrue and were started by someone with a grudge against her, but people are saying that* ***there's no smoke without fire****.*

Help

This proverb is often shortened to **no smoke without fire**:

♦ *We were all convinced that the rumours which were circulating about Lucy were lies, but it turned out to be a case of* ***no smoke without fire****. She hadn't been arrested for drink-driving, but she had been charged with dangerous driving.*

There is nothing new under the sun

However much you aim for novelty, everything has been done, said or seen before: ♦ *The young people think these very short skirts are the latest in fashion, but they were fashionable when their grandmothers were young;* ***there is nothing new under the sun****.* ♦ *Stella thought she was being innovative having her wedding reception in an underground cave. She was annoyed to discover that her cousin had done the same thing several years ago;* ***there is nothing new under the sun****.* ♦ *Frank said that he had come up with a completely new idea for a sci-fi novel. But when he told* *us the plot, I realized I had read a book like that last year;* ***there's nothing new under the sun****.*

Did you know?

The proverb has a biblical origin, being an allusion to Ecclesiastes 1:9—'There is no new thing under the sun.'

There is safety in numbers

If you are in a risky or dangerous situation, it is safer to be accompanied by several other people than to be alone: ♦ *It would be best if a whole group of us went to the boss to complain about the extra hours we're having to work rather than choosing one representative to do so;* ***there is safety in numbers*** *and he's likely to be very angry.* ♦ *The man holding the hostage was armed and the policeman who found him rightly decided that* ***there was safety in numbers*** *and phoned the station to ask for a backup team.* ♦ *Tom says that he is going out with several girls at once because* ***there is safety in numbers****. He's not planning to marry and he doesn't want any of them to get serious about him.*

Did you know?

The proverb may have a biblical origin. It may be a reference to Proverbs 11:14—'In the multitude of counsellors there is safety.'

There's many a slip 'twixt cup and lip

Similar

Don't count your chickens before they are hatched.

First catch your hare.

Several things can go wrong between the start and the end of a project. This is a warning against being over-confident: ♦ *Harry usually wins the annual golf tournament and he's so confident of winning again this year that he's already started planning a celebration party. However,* ***there's many a slip 'twixt cup and lip*** *and quite a few new young players have entered.* ♦ *Meg has handed in her notice to her employer although she hasn't yet had confirmation that she has got the job which she applied for.* ***There's many a slip 'twixt cup and lip*** *and* *she could find herself jobless.* ♦ *Bob's so sure that his father will lend him the money for the car that he has put a deposit on it. But* ***there's many a slip 'twixt cup and lip*** *and Bob's father said just a few weeks ago that Bob should stop borrowing from him and save up for what he wanted.*

Help

The proverb is sometimes shortened to **there's many a slip**:

♦ *Jackie is convinced that she can pass her exams and has arranged to spend the summer overseas. But* ***there's many a slip****; the exams were particularly difficult and, if she fails any of them, she'll have to be here to resit them.*

There's no fool like an old fool

You would expect people to become wiser as they grow older and gain more experience of life. This is, however, not always the case and some old people are more foolish than young people: ♦ *Helen is twenty-five years younger than Harry and it's quite obvious that she is just interested in his money. Yet Harry believes that she is in love with him and is planning to marry her;* ***there's no fool like an old fool****.* ♦ *Jim thinks that the young people who go around with him are interested in what he says about his sailing adventures and that they admire him for his sailing expertise. But they only stay friends with him in order to be allowed to sail his state-of-the-art boat and they laugh at him behind his back;* ***there's no fool like an old fool****.* ♦ *Meg spends a lot of money on make-up and designer clothes and believes that she looks younger than she really is, although, if anything, she looks older than she is;* ***there's no fool like an old fool****.*

There's no place like home

Wherever you may go, you always regard your home as a very special place where you feel at ease: ♦ *David had lived abroad for most of his working life,*

East, west, home's best.

but he decided to return to his homeland to retire; ***there's no place like home****, as they say.* ♦ *I was offered a job in the head office of the firm in New York, but I decided to stay here;* ***there's no place like home****, in my opinion.* ♦ *Even Mike, who enjoys travelling very much and has visited most countries in the world, agrees that* ***there's no place like home****.*

Did you know?

The proverb is a quotation from the words of a song 'Home Sweet Home' written by John Howard Payne for the musical play *Clari, the Maid of Milan,* first performed at Covent Garden in London in 1823—''Mid pleasure and palaces though we may roam, / Be it ever so humble, there's no place like home.'

There's none so blind as those who will not see

It is more difficult to get someone to be aware of, or understand, a situation if they refuse to do so and deliberately ignore it, than it is to get someone to understand a situation when they have difficulty in doing so: ♦ *If Jeff had looked at his bank statements he would have realized that he was in serious financial trouble, but* ***there's none so blind as those who will not see****.* ♦ *Pam must be aware that her fiancé is dating another woman, but* ***there's none so blind as those who will not see****.* ♦ ***There's none so blind as those who will not see****; Pat believes her son is being led astray by other boys, but everyone else knows he is the ringleader.*

Help

The proverb also occurs in the shorter form **none so blind as those who will not see**:

♦ *Doctors say that Bob should have been aware that there was something wrong with his heart, and we all think that it was a case of* ***none so blind as those who will not see****.*

A proverb with a similar meaning is **there's none so deaf as those who will not hear**:

♦ *Several people told Jean that they thought her son was playing truant, and yet she said that she was amazed when the school contacted her about this;* ***there's none so deaf as those who will not hear****.*

Those who live in glass houses shouldn't throw stones

You should not criticize or condemn other people if you could be open to criticism yourself, especially with reference to the same thing: ♦ *Mrs Smart was saying horrible things about Mrs Jackson, whose son has just gone to jail, but many of the older people in the town know that Mrs Smart's oldest son was convicted of robbery as a very young man;* ***those who live in glass houses shouldn't throw stones****.* ♦ *Lisa is condemning her granddaughter for wanting to get married at the age of 20, which Lisa thinks is too young, although she herself eloped to get married when she was 17;* ***those who live in glass houses shouldn't throw stones****.* ♦ *John's dad is very critical of him for failing one of his university exams, but Frank was at university with John's dad and said that he failed all his first-year exams;* ***those who live in glass houses shouldn't throw stones****.*

Help

A common alternative form of the proverb is **people in glass houses shouldn't throw stones**. It is a very common proverb and is often used in the shortened form **people in glass houses**:

♦ *I heard my next-door neighbour criticizing the state of my front garden and yet hers is overgrown and covered in weeds;* ***people in glass houses****.*

In this shortened form, the proverb has become a cliché.

Throw dirt enough, and some will stick

If enough bad things are said about a person, some of them will be believed and this will have a damaging effect on the person's reputation: ♦ *There have been a great many rumours about the politician's business affairs; it's not clear whether, in fact, he has done anything illegal, but you know what they say—* ***throw dirt enough, and some will stick****.* ♦ *People gossiped a lot about Sue because she flirted a lot with several of the men in the tennis club when her fiancé was overseas. Her behaviour was probably quite innocent, but, as the proverb says,* ***throw dirt enough, and some will stick****.* ♦ *None of the Jones family has ever been in trouble with the police, but their neighbours talk about the fact that they all seem to have a lot of money to spend, although not one of them has a job. It could all be just malicious gossip, but* ***throw dirt enough, and some will stick****.*

Help

An alternative version of this proverb is **throw mud enough, and some will stick** and this is often shortened to **mud sticks**:

♦ *Jack left his job very suddenly just after the police were called to the office to investigate a case of suspected theft and that sparked off a number of rumours; he may well not be connected with the theft, but* ***mud sticks****.*

Time and tide wait for no man

Similar

Make hay while the sun shines.

Strike while the iron is hot.

This proverb advises us to grasp opportunities as soon as they arise, rather than delay a decision, as time moves on and the opportunities might not be available for very long. It is often used to make someone come to a decision, and is used humorously sometimes by someone who is leaving somewhere: ♦ *You really will have to decide soon whether to accept the job offer or not, or it will be withdrawn;* ***time and tide wait for no man****.* ♦ *You must decide by tomorrow whether you want to buy my car or not;* ***time and tide wait for no man****.* ♦ *Well, it's been fun seeing you again, but I must go now;* ***time and tide wait for no man****, as they say.*

Time flies

Time passes extremely quickly: ♦ *I can't believe our holiday is nearly at an end;* ***time flies****.* ♦ *It seems hardly any time since the children were babies and now they're going to university;* ***time flies****.* ♦ ***Time flies****; I thought at the beginning of term that I had plenty of time to study for my exams, but now there's only a week left.*

Help

This is a very common proverb and it has become a cliché. It is a translation of the Latin phrase **tempus fugit** and this is also used as a proverb, sometimes humorously:

♦ ***Tempus fugit****; it's time that I got back to work.*

Time is a great healer

All things get better in time. This proverb is usually now used with reference to emotional pain and said in an attempt to make the suffering seem more bearable: ♦ *Pat is distraught at the death of her father, and she needs time to grieve, but* ***time is a great healer****.* ♦ *Tom thinks just now that he will never get over his wife leaving him, but* ***time is a great healer****.* ♦ *The death of a child is an appalling tragedy and the parents can hardly bear the pain, but* ***time is a great healer****.*

Similar

Time works wonders.

Help

An alternative form of the proverb is **time heals everything**, while variants of it include **time heals all things** and **time cures all things**.

Time is money

The idea behind this proverb is that people use time to work and earn money and so time is financially valuable: ♦ *The TV repair firm will say only that someone will call today, but I can't stay at home all day waiting for the mechanic;* ***time is money****.* ♦ *I have been on the phone for ages trying to get through to the right person to make* *a complaint about faulty goods. I do wish firms would realize that* ***time is money****. ♦ The old lady was shocked at the cost of the repair to her washing machine, but the mechanic spent quite a lot of time getting to her house and* ***time is money****.*

Time will tell

It will become clear at some point in the future what the truth of something is, whether something has been successful, etc: ♦ *We can't say at present whether the operation has improved the patient's condition, but* ***time will tell****. ♦ A great deal of money has been put into improving the educational system, but it is too soon to know how successful these improvements have been;* ***time will tell****. ♦ Sara says that she will easily be able to earn enough money to repay the loan on time, but* ***time will tell****.*

Help

An alternative form of this proverb is **only time will tell**:

♦ *The new drug may prove effective in treating the condition;* ***only time will tell****.*

Time works wonders

Similar

Time is a great healer.

The passage of time can have an amazing effect on situations or attitudes causing major change: ♦ *The two sisters were estranged when they were young after a bitter quarrel. But they became friends many years later when they met by chance and could scarcely remember what the quarrel had been about;* ***time works wonders****. ♦ Just now, the children resent the fact that their father is marrying again and is putting someone else in place of their beloved mother, but* ***time works wonders*** *and their attitude will change. ♦ Ten years ago, Julie was grief-stricken at the failure of her marriage and seemed to be facing a bleak future of unemployment and poverty. Now she owns a very* *successful business and is very happy in her second marriage;* ***time works wonders****.*

Times change and we with time

Things change with the passage of time and people's attitudes, beliefs, etc, change also: ♦ *My mother says that when she was a girl, very few ordinary families went out to eat, but nowadays many families regularly eat in restaurants:* ***times change and we with time****.* ♦ *Fifty years ago, women tended to marry quite young, some even in their teens, and have children right away after that. In this day and age, women tend to concentrate on their career when they are young, and postpone marriage and childbearing;* ***times change and we with time****.* ♦ *Just a few decades ago it was seen as a disgrace to be in debt, but now most of us have mortgages, bank loans and credit cards and wouldn't be able to function without debt;* ***times change and we with time****.*

To err is human

It is part of human nature to have faults and failings. This proverb is often used to try to persuade someone not to think too badly of someone who has done something wrong: ♦ *Certainly, Maggie should not have pretended to be sick and taken the day off school to go to a pop concert, but her favourite group were playing and* ***to err is human****.* ♦ *Tom should not have pretended to be older than he is in order to get into the cinema, but all his friends were going and they had been looking forward to seeing the film for ages. You would probably have done the same when you were young and* ***to err is human****.* ♦ *Alice lied when she said that she had previous experience of being a waitress, but she desperately needed the job to support her children and* ***to err is human****.*

Help

The longer, and now less common, form of this saying is **to err is human; to forgive, divine**, which means that it is part of human nature to have faults and failings and it is part of the nature of God to forgive these. (Although the idea that human error or sin is inevitable is a very old idea, being known in Roman times, it is Alexander Pope's *Essay on Criticism* (1711) that is the origin of the proverb—'Good nature and good sense must ever join: To err is human; to forgive, divine.')

To know all is to forgive all

Often, if you know all the details relating to a situation, you are less likely to blame or criticize someone for something: ♦ *People would stop criticizing Joan for not trying to get a job if she explained to them that she was seriously ill;* ***to know all is to forgive all***. ♦ *When the maid explained that she had taken some of the leftover food from the kitchen because her children were starving, her employer forgave her and said she could take the leftovers any time;* ***to know all is to forgive all***. ♦ *For years Pam blamed her mother for leaving her father until her aunt told her that her mother had been regularly badly beaten by him;* ***to know all is to forgive all***.

Tomorrow is another day

This optimistic proverb indicates that things might improve in the future and that you should put aside the problems of the present: ♦ *You may not have played very well today, but at least you got through to the next round and* ***tomorrow is another day***. ♦ *It's too bad that you didn't get the job, but* ***tomorrow is another day*** *and you still have several other interviews to attend.* ♦ *I don't think that I did very well in that exam, but* ***tomorrow is another day****, and I've studied more for the other exams.*

Did you know?

The original form of this proverb is **tomorrow is a new day**, which may have been translated from Spanish.

Tomorrow never comes

This proverb warns us against postponing things until another time because they may never get done: ♦ *Joe keeps saying that he will start revising for his exams tomorrow, but* ***tomorrow never comes****.* ♦ *You should start sorting out your financial affairs now. It's easier to put the task off until tomorrow, but* ***tomorrow never comes*** *and you will get further into debt.* ♦ *Every time I ring the painter and decorator he says that he will start work on my house tomorrow, but* ***tomorrow never comes****.*

Similar

Never put off till tomorrow what you can do today.

Procrastination is the thief of time.

Delays are dangerous.

Too many cooks spoil the broth

If there are too many people involved in a project, the project will not be as successful as it could be: ♦ *We need one person to make the final decision, because if we appoint a committee we will end up with disagreement and confusion;* ***too many cooks spoil the broth****.* ♦ *I think that we should leave Liz and Molly to organize the party and they can ask us for help if they need it;* ***too many cooks spoil the broth****.* ♦ *We have found that we need only three people to read the books and choose the winning novelist.* ***Too many cooks spoil the broth*** *and a larger team of judges causes delay, argument and ill feeling.*

Opposite

Two heads are better than one.

Many hands make light work.

Four eyes see more than two.

Help

The phrase **too many cooks** is also commonly used:

♦ *The protesters against the new office block are never going to achieve any success unless they appoint a strong leader to take charge because they are all squabbling amongst themselves instead of confronting the council; it's definitely a case of* ***too many cooks****.*

Travel broadens the mind

East, west, home's best.

Travel extends the range of people's knowledge by giving them experience of other cultures and customs: ♦ *Young people should be actively encouraged to take a year off between school and university in order to do some travelling;* ***travel broadens the mind****.* ♦ *Sam thinks that he has received a better education by working in various countries than he would have done if he had gone to university. He could well be right; after all,* ***travel broadens the mind****.* ♦ *It may be expensive, but we think it's important to take our children abroad on holiday every year because we firmly believe that* ***travel broadens the mind****.*

Truth is stranger than fiction

Things that happen in real life can be just as incredible and unexpected as imaginary events which are written about by fiction writers: ♦ *The child who came to live in the village last year turned out to be the daughter whom Jane had given up for adoption as a very young woman;* ***truth is stranger than fiction****.* ♦ *The tenant who had been so charming to us all was later found to have been a murderer who had escaped from prison;* ***truth is stranger than fiction****.* ♦ *We laughed when the children said that they had uncovered some buried treasure in the old house, but the police later identified it as the loot from a burglary which had taken place locally many years ago;* ***truth is stranger than fiction****.*

Two blacks don't make a white

Similar

Two wrongs don't make a right.

This proverb means the same as **two wrongs don't make a right**: ♦ *James may have damaged your car when he borrowed it, but it was wrong and foolish of you to damage his bike deliberately;* ***two blacks don't make a white****.*

Two heads are better than one

It helps to have another person's opinion or advice because they might think of something that you did not think of: ♦ *I'm going to ask Mary to help me draw up a menu for next week's dinner party;* ***two heads are better than one****.* ♦ *Janet is having problems with her teenage son and she's decided to discuss the matter with Fred.* ***Two heads are better than one*** *and Fred was a child psychologist before he retired.* ♦ *If you're having difficulty thinking what to buy Wendy as a wedding present, you should ask Pam for advice;* ***two heads are better than one*** *and she is one of Wendy's best friends.*

Similar

Four eyes see more than two.

Many hands make light work.

Opposite

Too many cooks spoil the broth.

Two is company, three is none

If a third person is present, it prevents the other two from enjoying each other's company as much as they would if the third person were not present. This proverb is used especially when two of the people concerned have a romantic relationship with each other: ♦ *John and Mary had not seen each other all week and were longing to be alone together. Unfortunately, Mary's sister didn't seem to realize that in such a situation* ***two is company and three is none****, and kept chatting away to them.* ♦ *Harry and Meg were disappointed when Meg's mother asked them to take Meg's little brother to the cinema with them;* ***two is company and three is none****, but they couldn't refuse.* ♦ *Molly was unaware that George and Lucy were romantically involved when she went out for a meal with them. Still, she quickly realized that it was a case of* ***two is company, three is none****, and left the restaurant as soon as she could.*

Help

A modern, more informal version of this proverb is **two's company, three's a crowd**.

Two of a trade never agree

Two people who work in the same trade or profession rarely agree with each other's opinion: ♦ *I asked one architect if it would be possible to add a room to the top of the house and he said no, but the next one I asked said that there would be no problem in doing so:* ***two of a trade never agree****.* ♦ *I'm not surprised that two different doctors gave you two different opinions on the seriousness of your condition;* ***two of a trade never agree****.* ♦ *Pamela needed some expert advice on what would be the best flowering plants to grow in her garden and she got completely conflicting advice from two professional gardeners;* ***two of a trade never agree****.*

Two wrongs don't make a right

If a wrong action is committed, this is no justification for a second wrong action being committed. The second wrong will not improve the situation even if it is committed as an act of revenge for the first wrong action: ♦ *You should not have attacked Jimmy and fought with him even if he did call you names;* ***two wrongs don't make a right****.* ♦ *The fact that Harry will not repay the money he owes you does not excuse you for deliberately damaging his car;* ***two wrongs don't make a right****, and now you are in deep trouble with the law.* ♦ *Julie thinks that she was fully justified in cutting up all Joan's clothes because Joan went out last week with Julie's boyfriend, but* ***two wrongs don't make a right****, and she has lost her boyfriend for being such a vengeful woman.*

Help

A variant of this proverb is **two blacks don't make a white**.

U

Union is strength

People and groups are more likely to be successful if they act together, rather than separately: ♦ *All the protesters against developing the park into a hotel and shopping complex should get together and agree on a letter to send to the town council;* ***union is strength****.* ♦ *The new manager is treating us all extremely badly, but instead of complaining to the boss individually, we should ask to speak to him as a group;* ***union is strength****.* ♦ *Several parents have complained individually to the head teacher about the lack of extracurricular activities and library facilities. However, parents would have more influence if they all asked for a meeting with him;* ***union is strength****.*

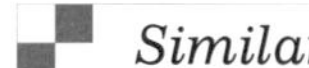

Similar

United we stand, divided we fall.

A house divided cannot stand.

Help

An alternative form of this proverb is **unity is strength**, which has the same meaning.

United we stand, divided we fall

This proverb emphasizes the success that people and groups can achieve if they act together, and the failure which is likely to occur if they act singly: ♦ *The new supervisor is a real bully and I think that we should tell him how we feel as a group;* ***united we stand, divided we fall****.* ♦ *There are some British politicians who are anti-Europe, but a great many of them are of the opinion that Britain should play a full part in the European Commission, and we think that they are right;* ***united we stand, divided we fall****.* ♦ *Neither Mum nor any of the rest of the family wants to go to our holiday cottage in the summer, and Mum thinks that we should all go and see Dad and try to persuade him to agree to go somewhere different; she says that it is a case of* ***united we stand, divided we fall****.* See also **divide and rule**.

Similar

Union is strength.

A house divided cannot stand.

V

Variety is the spice of life

Similar

A change is as good as a rest.

It takes all sorts to make a world.

Change and variation make life more interesting and enjoyable: ♦ *Jim says that **variety is the spice of life** and that he never stays in the same job for more than a few months.* ♦ *We've never been to the same holiday destination more than once; **variety is the spice of life**, as far as we're concerned.* ♦ *Alice and Mike tend to go to the same few restaurants. But the city is full of ethnic restaurants and Anna and Mark have tried most of them on the basis that **variety is the spice of life**.*

Virtue is its own reward

The satisfaction which comes from knowing that you have done the right thing is sufficient reward: ♦ *James might have got a medal for bravery or a reward from the parents, when he rescued the drowning boy from the river, but he refused to give his name. He's the kind of person who thinks that **virtue is its own reward**.* ♦ *We tried unsuccessfully to persuade our two teenagers that **virtue is its own reward**, when we asked them to babysit our friend's children while we went out with her; we had to pay them.* ♦ *I'm sure that Helen can't have been involved in rescuing people from the fire or her name would be given in the newspaper. She is certainly not the kind of person who thinks that **virtue is its own reward** and she loves publicity.*

W

Walls have ears

This is a warning to be careful what you say if you are talking about something confidential, because someone might overhear you, although you are not aware of them: ♦ *I'm in the office just now and **walls have ears**; I'll ring you again from home and tell you all about it.* ♦ *I thought Beth was being unduly cautious and suspicious by reminding me that **walls have ears**. However, I was glad I had not gone on with our private conversation when I opened the door and found the housekeeper standing behind it.* ♦ *Mary said that she didn't see anyone close by when she told her husband that she is pregnant. Yet someone must have heard it because the news is all round the office already; **walls have ears**.*

Similar

Little pitchers have big ears.

Help

This is a very common proverb which has become a cliché.

Waste not, want not

This proverb advocates thrift. If you do not squander your money or resources, you will never be in need: ♦ *You should use the chicken carcass to make stock for soup instead of throwing it out; **waste not, want not**.* ♦ *My grandmother says that when she was young, it was a case of **waste not, want not**. People mended or darned their clothes when they needed repairing, instead of throwing them out, as we do nowadays.* ♦ ***Waste not, want not**; if the children have smaller helpings, they're more likely to finish their food and then it won't have to go in the bin.*

We must learn to walk before we can run

This proverb advises us to have patience and not try to do ambitious, advanced things before we have some experience of the elementary or simpler stages: ♦ ***We must learn to walk before we can run**; if you want to play the piano properly you must practise* *scales and not try to play tunes right away.* ♦ *Someone ought to tell James that* **we must learn to walk before we can run**; *he wasn't listening to any of the theory which he was being taught about driving a car during his first lesson, but just wanted to start the engine and get going.* ♦ *Frank assumed that he would start in a management position in the family firm, but his father reminded him that* **we must learn to walk before we can run** *and said that he had to gain experience of all the departments, including the factory.*

Help

The phrase **run before you can walk** is also commonly used:

♦ *Pat was not nearly experienced enough to apply for such a job; he was trying to* **run before he could walk**.

An early, now archaic, form of the proverb was **we must creep before we can go**.

Well begun is half done

Similar

A good beginning makes a good ending.

It is the first step that is difficult.

If a job, project, etc, is carried out properly from the start, the job will take less time than it otherwise would: ♦ *The contractors have already laid the foundations of the new building and are ahead of schedule; let us hope that it is a case of* **well begun is half done**. ♦ *We are hopeful that it will not take us too long to collect enough money for the renovation of the church hall because we've been very successful in the first few months of our appeal. We hope that it will be a case of* **well begun is half done**. ♦ **Well begun is half done**, *hopefully, and this year's batch of students appear to have appreciated the need for hard work right from the beginning.*

What can't be cured must be endured

If something cannot be got rid of, you just have to put up with it: ♦ *Jean and her husband find it very difficult looking after her elderly parents as well as their young children, but there is no one else who can help, and, as*

Jean says, ***what can't be cured must be endured****. ♦ The flat which Mary and Tom rent is really far too small for them and their children, but it's all they can afford and* ***what can't be cured must be endured****. ♦ Peter's father has been ill for some time and is now bedridden, but he accepts the situation with resignation, saying that* ***what can't be cured must be endured****.*

What the eye doesn't see, the heart doesn't grieve over

You cannot get upset about something if you do not know about it: ♦ *I'm not going to tell Dad that Jack borrowed the car without his permission; he would be very angry if he knew, but* ***what the eye doesn't see, the heart doesn't grieve over****. ♦ Molly's dog nearly got run over by a car when Sue was taking it for a walk, but Sue has decided not to mention the incident to Molly on the grounds that* ***what the eye doesn't see, the heart doesn't grieve over****. ♦ One of Anne's plants died when I was looking after her house, but I bought one that looks exactly the same and she'll never know the difference;* ***what the eye doesn't see, the heart doesn't grieve over****.*

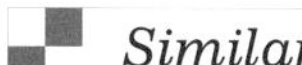

Similar

Ignorance is bliss.

What you don't know can't hurt you.

What you don't know can't hurt you

This proverb emphasizes the advantage of ignorance in certain situations: ♦ *You may suspect that your boss is not telling the truth when he fills in his tax returns, but it is best not to know the details;* ***what you don't know can't hurt you****. ♦ Pete's wife was telling the police the truth when she told them that she did not know anything about his housebreaking activities; he was always of the opinion that* ***what you don't know can't hurt you****. ♦ Police interviewed Pam's employees when investigating a claim that her firm was engaged in illegal money laundering, but it was a case of* ***what you don't know can't hurt you****. They could tell them very little about the business operation, since Pam kept most of the information to herself.*

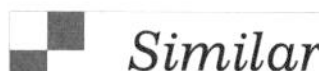

Similar

Ignorance is bliss.

What the eye doesn't see, the heart doesn't grieve over.

What you lose on the swings you gain on the roundabouts

Overall, your gains and losses, or advantages and disadvantages, tend to end up being the same and so balance out: ♦ *The cost of getting to your holiday destination is quite high, but the cost of living is very cheap there;* ***what you lose on the swings you gain on the roundabouts****.* ♦ *This sweater is more expensive than the other one, but it is of better quality and will last much longer;* ***what you lose on the swings you gain on the roundabouts****.* ♦ *We might lose some sales if we close the shop on Mondays, but we will save on salaries for sales staff;* ***what you lose on the swings you gain on the roundabouts****.*

Help

The proverb is sometimes shortened to **what you lose on the swings**:

♦ *The distance from here to the holiday cottage is shorter if you go through town, rather than by the coast road, but the traffic will be heavy in town at this time of day and it will be a case of* ***what you lose on the swings****.*

Sometimes the idea expressed by the proverb is contained in the idiomatic expression **it's swings and roundabouts**:

♦ ***It's swings and roundabouts*** *which supermarket you shop at; some things are cheaper at one and some are more expensive, and vice versa.*

An alternative form of the proverb is **what you lose on the roundabouts you gain on the swings**.

Did you know?

The proverb has its origin in the fairground. Some days a fairground owner might make more money from operating the swings, and some days he might make more money from operating the roundabouts.

What you've never had, you never miss

If you have never been in possession of something, or known what it was like to have something, then you cannot feel a sense of loss at not having it: ♦ *Lucy's father was very wealthy and her family were devastated when he lost a great deal of money in the recession. On the other hand, Tim's family didn't have any money, and were largely unaffected by the recession. It was a case of* ***what you've never had, you never miss****.* ♦ *Grace feels sad that she is getting older and losing her beauty, but Molly said that she herself was never beautiful, anyway, and that* ***what you've never had, you never miss****.* ♦ *The Wilson family have recently moved here from the city and they keep asking us if we don't miss the theatre and art galleries, but we have lived all our lives in this small town and have never known such facilities;* ***what you've never had, you never miss****.*

Similar

You cannot lose what you never had.

Help

An alternative form of this proverb is **you never miss what you've never had**.

What's bred in the bone will come out in the flesh

Inherited characteristics or family traits cannot be concealed and soon become obvious: ♦ *James has decided to go to agricultural college; all his family are farmers and* ***what's bred in the bone comes out in the flesh****.* ♦ *Paul and Nora are both doctors, as were both Paul's parents, and they assumed that their daughter would want to study medicine also. But it wasn't a case of* ***what's bred in the bone comes out in the flesh****; she decided to be a journalist.* ♦ *I'm not surprised that Rob doesn't want to find a job because his whole family are lazy creatures;* ***what's bred in the bone will come out in the flesh****.*

Similar

Blood will tell.

The apple never falls far from the tree.

Help

The proverb is often found in the shortened form **what's bred in the bone**:

♦ *I'm not surprised that Bob has topped his class because his whole family are extremely high achievers;* ***what's bred in the bone****.*

What's done cannot be undone

Similar

It's no use crying over spilt milk.

This proverb is used to emphasize that there is no point in spending time in regretting or worrying about something that you cannot undo or change, however sorry you are: ♦ *It's unfortunate that you quarrelled with Jim just before he died, but* ***what's done cannot be undone****, and you must just concentrate on remembering all the good times which you and he had together.* ♦ *Allan worked very hard at making his new business a success and he is devastated that it has failed, but* ***what's done cannot be undone*** *and he should now be making plans for the future.* ♦ *Pam feels very bad about running over the dog in the street and says that she will never drive again, but* ***what's done cannot be undone*** *and she cannot get to work by public transport.*

Help

A less formal form of this proverb is **what's done is done**:

♦ *Jim says that he feels that he made a mistake in breaking up with Anne, but she has now married someone else and Jim must just forget about her;* ***what's done is done****.*

The proverb, particularly in its less formal form, has become a cliché.

What's sauce for the goose is sauce for the gander

What is considered acceptable for one person should be considered acceptable for someone else in a similar situation. This proverb advocates equality, originally between the sexes, but now on a wider scale: ♦ *It's only fair that Jim should share the childcare with Beth because they're both working full-time;* ***what's sauce for the goose is sauce for the***

gander. ♦ *The rest of the teachers have to put up with having no place to park and so there is no reason why the new gym building should include parking places for the PE staff;* ***what's sauce for the goose is sauce for the gander***. ♦ *The chief executive should not get a salary increase this year if the workers have to accept a pay freeze;* ***what's sauce for the goose is sauce for the gander***.

Help

The word 'gander' is the name given to a male goose, the proverb originally being a plea for women to be treated equally with men. The proverb literally means that a sauce which would be suitable for serving with a female goose would also be suitable for serving with a male goose.

When in Rome, do as the Romans do

When you are in another country or somewhere where people have different customs from you or behave differently from you, you should copy their manners, customs, etc: ♦ *Women here cover their heads when they go to church and you should do the same;* ***when in Rome, do as the Romans do***. ♦ *It's the custom there for dinner guests to arrive exactly on time and so we mustn't do what we would do in Britain and arrive about 15 minutes late;* ***when in Rome, do as the Romans do***. ♦ *I have been living in southern Spain for a few months and now take a siesta in the middle of the day and work late. It's a case of* ***when in Rome, do as the Romans do****, and it is a custom I very much approve of.*

Help

The proverb is often shortened to **when in Rome**:

♦ *I would have liked a glass of wine, but I abstained because I was the guest of an Arab family who did not take alcohol;* ***when in Rome***.

Particularly in the shortened form, the proverb has become a cliché.

Did you know?

The proverb is said to have its origin in a saying by St Ambrose (*c* 340–97). This saying was a reply to a problem put to him by St Augustine. When St Monica, the mother of St Augustine, visited her son in Milan, she was puzzled to find that the church there did not fast on Saturdays, although the church in Rome did. She asked her son how she should act and he asked St Ambrose's advice, hence his reply.

When one door shuts, another opens

Opposite

Opportunity never knocks twice.

This optimistic proverb suggests that another opportunity is likely to occur if you lose one: ♦ *Jane was really upset when she was declared redundant, but the very next week she was offered a much better post in a larger firm;* ***when one door shuts, another opens****.* ♦ *George's application to the local university was rejected, but he was later offered a place at a much more prestigious one;* ***when one door shuts, another opens****.* ♦ *Rose was very upset when Ron broke off their engagement, but a few months later she met Mark, with whom she is very happy;* ***when one door shuts, another opens****.*

Help

An alternative form of this proverb is **when one door closes, another opens**, and 'as' is sometimes substituted for 'when' in both forms.

When poverty comes in at the door, love flies out of the window

When people who are in love experience poverty, their love for each other comes to an end. This proverb is used to emphasize the strain which not having enough money can put on a relationship: ♦ *John and Sheila were very happy when they were first married and had plenty of money with both of them working. But they began to quarrel bitterly when Shelia had to give up work when the twins were born; sadly, it was a case of* ***when poverty comes in at the door, love flies out of the window****.* ♦ *George says that he puts the break-up of his marriage down to the loss of his job;* ***when poverty comes in at the door, love flies out of the window*** *and his wife was not prepared to put up with living on unemployment benefit.* ♦ *Jean had assumed that Henry would inherit a great deal of property on his father's death, and when she discovered that it would all go to Henry's elder brother, she broke off their engagement;* ***when poverty comes in at the door, love flies out of the window****.*

When the cat's away, the mice will play

When someone in authority is not present, those whom the person is in charge of will take advantage of the situation in some way, such as by playing or enjoying themselves instead of working: ♦ *The manager was off sick and the office workers were sitting around chatting and drinking coffee;* ***when the cat's away the mice will play****.* ♦ *As soon as Dan heard that his parents were going away for the weekend, he decided to have a party and invite all his friends;* ***when the cat's away, the mice will play****.* ♦ ***When the cat's away, the mice will play****; I'm not surprised that the children were making so much noise while the teacher was out of the room.*

Help

This is a very common proverb and it often appears in the shortened form **when the cat's away**, which has become a cliché:

♦ *The teacher was out of the room and the children were all calling out to each other and making a dreadful noise;* ***when the cat's away****, as they say.*

Did you know?

In origin, the proverb refers to the fact that, in the absence of a cat, the mice will come out of their holes and scamper around, although they would not dare do this if the cat were present.

Where there's a will, there's a way

If someone is determined enough to do something, he or she will find some means of doing it: ♦ *Mary comes from a poor family, but she is quite determined to go to university and I am certain that she will get there;* ***where there's a will, there's a way.*** ♦ ***Where there's a will, there's a way;*** *if Liz really loves Bill, she will marry him, whether her parents object or not.* ♦ *It's going to be very difficult to get enough money together to renovate the old building, but* ***where there's a will, there's a way;*** *we are all very enthusiastic about the project and hope to get it underway.*

While there's life, there's hope

Similar

Hope springs eternal.

A drowning man will clutch at a straw.

If a person is still alive, he or she can hope to survive. The proverb is usually used when someone is ill, injured or in danger: ♦ *The rescuers are having difficulty in reaching the climber and he is badly injured, but* ***while there's life, there's hope.*** ♦ *The survivor of the accident is having major surgery and she is in a very weak state, but* ***while there's life, there's hope.*** ♦ *The child is very ill with a serious infection of the brain and her parents have been told that she might die; still,* ***while there's life, there's hope.***

Why keep a dog and bark yourself?

There is no point in employing someone to do something if you are going to do the work yourself: ♦ *It's ridiculous that Lucy pays a gardener to look after her garden and yet does such a lot of gardening herself;* ***why keep a dog and bark yourself?*** ♦ *Mary is foolish to tidy the house before the cleaner gets there;* ***why keep a dog and bark yourself?*** ♦ *I don't understand why James prefers to drive himself, rather than let his chauffeur drive;* ***why keep a dog and bark yourself?***

You are never too old to learn

People are never too old to learn something new: ♦ *Beth's grandmother firmly believes that* ***you are never too old to learn****; she is 70 years old and has just started swimming lessons.* ♦ *It's a good idea for Dad to take a creative writing course after he retires; he has always wanted to be a writer and* ***you are never too old to learn.*** ♦ *Harry says that* ***you are never too old to learn*** *and is sending all his older workers on a computer course.*

 *Opposite*

You can't teach an old dog new tricks.

Old habits die hard.

Help

An alternative form of this proverb is **it is never too late too learn**:

♦ *Julie was hesitant about going to university after she retired because she was so much older than even the most mature of the rest of the students. But as she said herself,* ***it is never too late to learn****.*

You are what you eat

The kind of food you eat has an important effect on the kind of person you are. This proverb is particularly popular in modern times when doctors have discovered that the kind of food we eat can have a major effect on both our short-term and long-term health: ♦ *Jane always looks pale and ill, but* ***you are what you eat*** *and she never bothers to eat proper meals.* ♦ ***You are what you eat*** *and I know that it is important for the children to eat lots of green vegetables. Unfortunately, they much prefer hamburgers and chips.* ♦ ***You are what you eat*** *and Jim should give up eating so much fat; he's already had a minor heart attack.*

Did you know?

The origin of the saying is uncertain, but it is sometimes attributed to Anthelme Brillat-Savarin (1755–1826), who wrote in his classic book *Physiology of Taste* (1825): 'Tell me what you eat and I will tell you what you are.'

You can have too much of a good thing

You can have an excess even of things which you like very much because you may get tired and bored with them: ♦ *Bob used to long for more leisure time before he retired, but now that he has retired, he doesn't know what to do with all his leisure; it's true that* ***you can have too much of a good thing***. ♦ *When we first went to work abroad, we thought that we would love living in a warm, sunny climate, but we found it much too hot and even found ourselves missing the cold and rain of home;* ***you can have too much of a good thing***. ♦ *Pam and Billy went to live in the country because they wanted peace and quiet and were tired of the bustle and noise of city life. They soon found that* ***you can have too much of a good thing*** *and found the country too quiet and dull.*

You can only die once

This proverb is used to bring supposed consolation to someone who is in great danger or difficulty. It is sometimes used humorously: ♦ *The soldiers were about to be engaged in a battle which was likely to be long and involve much loss of life. Their commanding officer gave them some last words of comfort including '***You can only die once***'.* ♦ *The old man was in the terminal stages of cancer and told the doctors that he was now more afraid of pain than death; '***You can only die once***,' he said, 'but pain can last a long time.'* ♦ *We telephoned my brother to say that our car was stuck in a snowdrift and that we were very cold and hungry. It didn't help at all when he replied, 'Don't worry,* ***you can only die once***!'

Help

Another version of this proverb is **a man can die but once**.

You can take a horse to the water, but you can't make it drink

You can give someone the opportunity to do something, but you cannot force them to do it, if they are determined not to do so: ♦ *Teachers can recommend books to students, but they cannot force them to read them;* ***you can take a horse to the water, but you can't make it drink.*** ♦ *The school's career advisor has a great deal of useful advice to offer students, but she cannot compel them to act on her advice;* ***you can take a horse to the water, but you can't make it drink.*** ♦ *The doctor has drawn up a healthy diet for Bill, but he ignores it and keeps on eating chips and junk food;* ***you can take a horse to the water, but you can't make it drink.***

Help

The 'the' is sometimes omitted from the proverb: **you can take a horse to water, but you can't make it drink**; and 'lead' is sometimes substituted for 'take': **you can lead a horse to (the) water, but you can't make it drink.**

You cannot get blood from a stone

You cannot get money from someone who does not have any, or from someone who is too mean to give you any: ♦ *Jim owes Molly some money and she is trying unsuccessfully to get it back; Jim is always penniless these days and* ***you can't get blood from a stone.*** ♦ *One of Pete's customers has not paid him for the building work he did, but Pete has decided not to sue him on the grounds that* ***you cannot get blood from a stone****. Apparently, unknown to Pete, the man has very little money and could not really afford the building repairs.* ♦ *We suggested to Jenny that she ask her grandfather to give her some money towards her college expenses, but Jenny says that he's a real miser and that it would be like* ***getting blood from a stone****.*

Help

An old version of the proverb is **you cannot get blood out of a turnip**.

You cannot have it both ways

Similar

You cannot have your cake and eat it.

You cannot expect to have the advantages of two opposing courses of action; you have to choose one course of action and accept the consequences: ♦ *If Anna wants to have more money, she will have to give up part-time work and start working full-time;* ***she cannot have it both ways****.* ♦ *Pam cannot be a full-time mother and have a full-time career;* ***she cannot have it both ways*** *and must make a decision.* ♦ *Pete wants to be his own boss and work freelance, but he also wants the security of a regular salary. Unfortunately,* ***he cannot have it both ways****.*

You cannot have your cake and eat it

Similar

You cannot have it both ways.

It is not possible to use something and still to have it; you cannot have the advantages of alternative, and opposing, courses of action: ♦ *If you spend your money on new clothes, you won't be able to save enough money to go on holiday;* ***you cannot have your cake and eat it****.* ♦ ***You cannot have our cake and eat it****; it is not possible to use all the natural resources of the planet and still preserve the environment as we know it.* ♦ *People want excellent public services, but they do not want to pay increased taxes; alas,* ***you cannot have your cake and eat it****.*

Help

The proverb sometimes takes the form **you cannot eat your cake and have it**.

You cannot lose what you never had

If you were never in possession of something, you cannot regret its loss. This proverb is often said to stop someone complaining about what they see as a loss: ♦ *Sam was talking at length about his sorrow at losing the fish which he nearly caught, but Bill told him to forget it, saying, '***You cannot lose what you never had***.'* ♦ *There is no point in regretting the money which you might have won on the horse which won the last race. Since you decided not to bet on it,* ***you cannot lose what you never had****.* ♦ *Beth's bid for the house was rejected and she says that she is so upset at losing it that she is refusing to look at any other; someone should tell her that* ***you cannot lose what you never had****.*

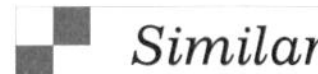

Similar

What you've never had, you never miss.

Help

A slightly older form of this proverb is **no man can lose what he never had**.

You cannot make an omelette without breaking eggs

Nothing can be achieved without some damage, accident or losses occurring, often to other people: ♦ *Bill says that* ***you cannot make an omelette without breaking eggs****. The firm needs to be slimmed down in order to be profitable and that, sadly, means making some of the workers redundant.* ♦ *Inevitably there will be some casualties if we go to war, although we hope that these will be minimal;* ***you cannot make an omelette without breaking eggs****.* ♦ *A remedy must be found for the level of traffic congestion in the city. As part of this remedy, the council has decided to pedestrianize the city centre; many of the retailers are not happy about this, but* ***you cannot make an omelette without breaking eggs****.*

Did you know?

This is a translation of an old French saying which might, it is claimed, have been popularized by Napoleon.

You cannot make bricks without straw

You cannot do a job properly without suitable equipment, material or resources: ♦ *Alice has been asked to start a new departmental library, but the budget she has been given will not buy nearly enough books; she says that* ***she*** *simply* ***cannot make bricks without straw****.* ♦ *Sam is very keen on DIY, but he tries to tackle some quite ambitious jobs without the right tools; we should really tell him that* ***you cannot make bricks without straw****.* ♦ *Jill is planning to open an antique shop, but she has neither enough stock nor enough money to buy more stock;* ***you cannot make bricks without straw****.*

Help

This is a very common proverb and sometimes the phrase **make bricks without straw** is used on its own: ♦ *Telling these poverty-stricken mothers to eat a proper, nutritious diet is telling them to* ***make bricks without straw****; all their money goes towards feeding and clothing their children.*

Did you know?

The proverb is biblical in origin, being a reference to Exodus 5:7—'Ye shall no more give the people straw to make brick, as heretofore; let them go and gather straw for themselves.'

You cannot put a quart into a pint pot

There is a limit to how much you can put into the space or time that is available to you and you should not try to get too much in; you should not try to do the impossible: ♦ *I would love to invite my friends to stay, but this house is scarcely big enough for my family;* ***you cannot put a quart into a pint pot****.* ♦ *A lot of people who have applied for tickets for the concert will not get them. It's a small hall and* ***you cannot put a quart into a pint pot****.* ♦ *The boss thinks that I can do all this work in a day, but there's about a week's work here and* ***you cannot put a quart into a pint pot****.*

Did you know?

A quart is a quarter of a gallon and equal to two pints.

You cannot put an old head on young shoulders

You cannot expect young people to have the experience and wisdom that people acquire as they get older: ♦ *Tom's teachers are trying to dissuade him from taking up acting as a career. They urge him to study law at university because this will lead to a secure, well-paid job, but Tom has chosen to ignore their advice;* ***you cannot put an old head on young shoulders****.* ♦ *Joe's grandfather said that Joe and his friends don't appreciate the value of the educational opportunities that have been given to them and that they should study more instead of partying. He should realize that that is the way of youth and that* ***you cannot put an old head on young shoulders****.*

You can't make a silk purse out of a sow's ear

It is impossible to make something fine or excellent out of poor materials. This proverb is sometimes used with reference to a person: ♦ *The bride-to-be has chosen a pattern for a very elegant dress for her wedding day, but has provided the dressmaker with material of very poor quality. The dressmaker has said that it can't be done as* ***you can't make a silk purse out of a sow's ear****.* ♦ *Helen wants very much to be a professional musician and she has spent a lot of money on the best of teachers. But she is wasting her money;* ***you cannot make a silk purse out of a sow's ear****.* ♦ *The teacher commented to a colleague that* ***you couldn't make a silk purse out of a sow's ear*** *when the father of one of his less bright pupils said that he hoped that the school would get his daughter into university.*

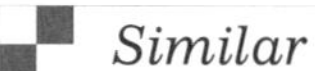

You cannot make bricks without straw.

Help

The word 'sow' is the name given to a female pig and pigs have very rough, bristly ears.

You can't please everyone

This proverb emphasizes the impossibility of getting everybody to approve of your actions: ♦ *Your parents and teachers are giving you conflicting advice and you should just decide what you want to do;* ***you can't please everyone****.* ♦ *It's certainly true that* ***you can't please everyone****; I was asked by the committee to choose a suitable venue for the concert, but at least half of them complained about my choice.* ♦ *Mark and a group of his friends decided to take a large holiday house together, but he has given up the idea because he couldn't get them to agree on a location;* ***you can't please everyone****.*

Help

An earlier form of this proverb was **you cannot please all men**. A modern variant is **you can't please everyone all of the time**.

You can't put new wine in old bottles

You cannot successfully introduce new ideas or policies into the framework of an old system or organization: ♦ *Pam tried to introduce some innovations into the old-fashioned accounting system, but her attempts didn't work;* ***you can't put new wine in old bottles****.* ♦ *Meg and Jack have bought a new house and furnished it with large pieces of old-fashioned furniture from Meg's parents' house and it looks all wrong;* ***you can't put new wine in old bottles****.* ♦ *The government would be better to reform the educational system completely, rather than try to bring a few new policies into the old-fashioned, existing system;* ***you can't put new wine in old bottles****.*

Did you know?

The origin of the proverb is biblical, being an allusion to Matthew 9:17—'Neither do men put new wine into old bottles: else the bottles break, and the wine runneth out, and the bottles perish.'

You can't teach an old dog new tricks

It is difficult to persuade older people to use new methods, acquire new skills or try out new ideas: ♦ *Molly was a few years off retirement age when the office was computerized, but she decided to leave at that point, saying that* ***you can't teach an old dog new tricks****.* ♦ ***You can't teach an old dog new tricks****; Mum says that she is quite happy to use her old traditional oven and she does not want a microwave one.* ♦ *Bob says that* ***you can't teach an old dog new tricks*** *and, anyway, he prefers to look up things in reference books than to search for material on the Internet.*

Similar

Old habits die hard.

Opposite

You are never too old to learn.

You can't tell a book by its cover

You cannot assess or judge what someone is like from their appearance: ♦ *Diana's parents were horrified when they met her new boyfriend, because he had long hair and was dressed in old, ragged jeans and a grubby sweater, but her grandmother said to them that* ***they could not tell a book by its cover****.* ♦ *It's important for candidates to dress smartly for job interviews, but it's also important for the interviewers to remember that* ***you can't tell a book by its cover****.* ♦ *The woman was very shabbily dressed and the students thought she was one of the cleaners, but, in fact, she was a senior lecturer in the English Department;* ***you can't tell a book by its cover****.*

Similar

Appearances are deceptive.

All that glitters is not gold.

Help

An alternative form of this proverb is **you can't judge a book by its cover**.

You can't win them all

This philosophical proverb acknowledges that you cannot be lucky or successful all the time. It is often used by someone who has just lost in order to account for his or her failure: ♦ *I lost to Jim at chess last night, but I'm not disappointed because I won all my other matches and* ***you can't win them all****.* ♦ *We've always had delicious food at that restaurant, but the meal last night was disappointing; ah well,* ***you can't win them all****.* ♦ *In previous years we've had lovely sunny weather for our annual fete, but this year, we had heavy rain;* ***you can't win them all****.*

Help

The proverb has been very commonly used, often in the form of **you can't win 'em all**, and has become a cliché.

You never know what you can do until you try

This proverb urges people to attempt things, even if they think that they will not be successful, since people are often capable of more than they think: ♦ *Paul's father thought that he would never be able to work a computer. But after a few lessons from Paul, he found that he was very good at it;* ***you never know what you can do until you try****.* ♦ *If you've never been on a skiing holiday, you should accept the invitation, even if you've never skied before;* ***you never know what you can do until you try****.* ♦ *Jean's father always said that* ***you never know what you can do until you try*** *and encouraged her to learn to drive, even though she was very nervous of cars.*

You never miss the water till the well runs dry

We tend to take certain things or certain people for granted and do not realize how much we need them until they are not there any more: ♦ *We didn't realize how much work the caretaker did in the factory until he retired:* ***you never miss the water till the well runs dry.*** ♦ ***You never miss the water until the well runs dry*** *and the Jacksons really did not appreciate their nanny's role in their children's lives until she gave in her notice and left.* ♦ *The local residents do most of their shopping in the supermarket and did not realize how much they relied on the local shop until it closed because of lack of business;* ***you never miss the water till the well runs dry.***

You scratch my back and I'll scratch yours

If you do me a favour or give me some help, I will do you a favour or give you some help in return. The proverb is often used with reference to something not completely honest: ♦ *He belongs to a group of businessmen who all went to school with each other and are always doing each other favours. It's a case of* ***you scratch my back and I'll scratch yours.*** ♦ *I heard that Henry was accepted as a member of the golf club because he gave the president's daughter a job in his firm;* ***you scratch my back and I'll scratch yours****, as they say.* ♦ *In most professions there is an element of* ***you scratch my back and I'll scratch yours.***

Similar

One good turn deserves another.

You should practise what you preach

If you are going to advise other people what to do, you should follow this advice yourself: ♦ ***You should practise what you preach****; our doctor gave my father a lecture about the dangers of smoking, but he smokes heavily himself.* ♦ *I heard you reprimanding the office junior for being a few minutes late, but you are rarely on time yourself;* ***you should practise what you preach.*** ♦ *It's a good thing to warn* *your son not to drive too fast, but* ***you should practise what you preach****; you always exceed the speed limit on the motorway.*

Help

The phrase **practise what you preach** is also frequently used in sentences:

♦ *If Dr Lamb* ***had practised what he preached*** *and not worked such long hours, he might have been alive today.*

♦ *Kathy was always talking about the importance of women's rights, but she certainly did not* ***practise what she preached****. In the factory which she owned, the male workers were paid more than the female ones.*

Proverbs in Context

Passage 1

Decision Time

Bob had a problem and it was one which he was finding very difficult to solve. He had just finished school and had planned to go straight to university in the autumn to study engineering. Now he wasn't so sure. He still wanted to study engineering, but he was thinking about deferring his university course.

He had just had a letter from his uncle Steve to say that his firm had transferred him to Australia for a year and Bob was very welcome to visit him. Furthermore, he might be able to help him find some work.

Bob was very tempted by the offer, but he was rather a cautious person by nature and was concerned about postponing his university place. He had inherited his caution from his mother, who was not at all happy about the possible Australian trip. She told Bob that he needed to find out far more details before coming to a decision. '**Look before you leap**' was her advice.

The trouble was that Bob did not have time to gather more information about the trip. It was a case of **he who hesitates is lost**, because his uncle had said that if he didn't hear from Bob more or less right away, he would assume that he wasn't interested and would offer the trip to one of his other nephews.

Bob's father, brother of Uncle Steve, was much more impulsive than his wife and son and his advice to Bob was to take advantage of what he saw as a golden opportunity. He said, 'You should **strike while the iron's hot** and phone Steve and accept. **Opportunity never knocks twice** and you'll regret it all your life if you don't take advantage of such a marvellous offer.'

Old habits die hard and still Bob was a bit uncertain. Most of his friends thought that he was mad even to consider refusing the offer. '**Nothing venture, nothing gain**,' said Terry, 'and think of all the marvellous experiences you'll have.'

'**Make hay while the sun shines**!' said Mike, Bob's elder brother. 'When you start work, you'll only get a few weeks' holiday a year. Travel now while you have the chance.'

Even the head teacher of Bob's school thought he should go, saying, It's not as if you have to choose between the trip and university. It's quite acceptable to postpone your course. In this case it's not true that **you cannot have your cake and eat it**. You can go to Australia and go to university. **All is grist that comes to the mill** and you should make the most of your opportunity.'

Time and tide wait for no man and it was decision time for Bob. Despite his caution, he decided to phone his uncle and accept. He never regretted the decision because he enjoyed his trip to Australia very much indeed.

Passage 2

A Search for Business Premises

Molly had been working as a dressmaker for a small fashion house for five years and was now tired of working for other people. She was a very confident person and had decided that it was time to start her own business. Now she was searching around for suitable premises.

'**First things first**,' warned Molly's father. 'Before you start looking at premises, you need to sort out the funding for this venture.'

'I was going to talk to you about that, Dad,' Molly said. 'I wonder if you could lend me the money to get me started.'

'**You cannot get blood from a stone**,' joked Molly's father. 'Don't forget your two brothers are still at university and they're costing me a lot of money. In any case, this is a professional venture and you should be professional about it. I'll help you draw up a business plan and you can take it to the bank. It'll take some time, but **if a thing's worth doing, it's worth doing well**.'

'But you always said "**Never a borrower nor a lender be**" when we were growing up,' replied Molly.

'That's true,' replied her father, 'but it doesn't apply to banks. Borrowing and lending are what banks are all about.'

Molly was not impressed at the length of time that the bank manager was taking to make up his mind. She was an impatient person and was anxious to have the business up and running. Knowing his daughter only too well, her father said, 'Try not be so impatient. **Rome wasn't built in a day**. It'll all be worth it if you get your business started.'

Soon, Molly got the decision from the bank and, to her joy, it was a positive one. Having organized the finances for her business, she now renewed her search for premises. She was depressed at the standard of the business accommodation that she could afford. 'I need premises which look smart and elegant to attract the right clientele,' said Molly, 'and everything I've seen is shabby and run-down.'

'You must **cut your coat according to your cloth**,' her father said. 'You can't afford flashy, expensive new premises just now. You should be able to find something in your price range that you can renovate to a reasonable standard.'

'**You can't make a silk purse out of a sow's ear**,' replied Molly. 'Nothing I've seen so far is even remotely suitable, even if I do renovate it. I know I haven't much money and **beggars can't be choosers**, but the places I've looked at have been terrible.'

'**Seek and ye shall find**,' replied her father. 'You haven't been looking very long and this is a big town. It might be an idea to get an estate agent's help. Meanwhile, don't give up. **Where there's a will, there's way**.'

Eventually Molly found something that met her high standards and soon her premises were open for business. 'I couldn't have done it without you, Dad,' she said, giving her father a hug.

Passage 3

Youth Crime

Police are expressing their concern about the number of crimes which are being committed by local youths. These crimes range from joyriding to serious burglary and assault and seem to be spiralling out of control.

Some local residents say that the rise in youth crime has been glaringly obvious for some time and that they have called for more police on the beat in the city centre. 'However,' said one of them, Joe Simon, yesterday, '**there's none so deaf as those who will not hear** and our requests have been ignored. They should lock up some of these louts who hang around street corners and that would lower the crime rate.'

A police spokesman explained, 'We can't lock up people who haven't done anything. Some of the youths may look scruffy and unkempt, but many of them are quite law-abiding. **You can't judge a book by its cover. Appearances are deceptive**.'

Joe Simon replied, 'A couple of them were arrested last week for car theft and they're all alike. **Birds of a feather flock together**. The police should at least disperse them when they see gangs of youths together.'

'I blame the parents,' said another resident, Margaret Smith. 'They've been too soft on these louts and have not disciplined them enough. **Spare the rod and spoil the child**. They should be taught that if you do wrong, you will be punished. **As you sow, so you reap**.'

One of the teachers at the local high school, James Brown, said, 'We should be careful not to condemn kids who have not done anything wrong just because they stand on street corners together. **Give a dog a bad name and you might as well hang him**. If we damage these kids' reputations now, it will affect them for life.'

'The answer to that is quite simple. Kids who are not wrongdoers must stop associating with those who are,' said Joe Simon. 'They must learn that **a man is known by the company he keeps**.'

Margaret Smith said, 'It would be a pity if innocent kids get a reputation for wrongdoing and this could happen, I know. **Throw enough mud, and some will stick**. However, we are all tired and nervous of all the youth crime that's taking place. **Desperate diseases must have desperate remedies**. If this means getting the police to disperse gangs of youths, then I'm in favour of it. At least we should give it a try.'

The police spokesman replied, 'If any of the youths do anything wrong, we can take action. Otherwise we are not empowered to do so. Those are the facts.'

Passage 4

A Cure for Misery

Pam was feeling and looking very miserable. The university vacation had just started and her boyfriend had just gone overseas to study for three months. At first, her friends had been sympathetic, but now she was beginning to annoy them, because she wouldn't do anything but mope about the place.

Anna lost patience with Pam first, saying to Mary, 'Her behaviour is ridiculous and I'm sure it's a case of **absence makes the heart grow fonder**. When they were together, they were always quarrelling.'

Mary replied, 'I think you're quite right. She's forgotten all Jack's many faults and is making a kind of saint out of him; **distance lends enchantment to the view**.'

'Well, I, for one, wish that it was a case of **out of sight, out of mind**,' commented Jane. 'She really is getting on my nerves. Why doesn't she get a vacation job like the rest of us? That would leave her less time to mope.'

'**Ask a silly question**!' replied Anna. 'Pam's father is so wealthy that she doesn't have to work. But you're right. She needs something to do. **The Devil finds work for idle hands to do**, as my grandmother says.'

'Her father won't let her work,' said Mary, 'but surely he wouldn't object if she did some voluntary work. A group of my friends are redecorating the local hostel for the homeless in their spare time this weekend and they need more people to get it finished on time. It's a case of **many hands make light work**. Pam won't have had any experience of that kind of work but she could do something and **every little helps**.'

'I think she'd be better at something more administrative and I know just the thing,' said Lucy. 'My mother works for a children's charity and they're organizing a charity ball. It's quite an upmarket affair and they need someone to sell tickets for it. Pam would be perfect because **birds of a feather flock together**. Being wealthy herself, she's bound to know a lot of affluent people who could afford to buy tickets.'

'**Money talks**, you mean,' said Anna cynically. 'I would much rather paint the hostel than sell tickets to the wealthy but **one man's meat is another man's poison** and I'm sure that Pam would prefer the charity ball. Let's ask her.'

Pam rather reluctantly agreed to be on the charity ball committee, and found she enjoyed it very much. Having something to do did, indeed, take her mind off her misery and her absent boyfriend—so much so that she started going out with someone else while Jack was still away.

Passage 5

Preparing a Protest

Many people were very angry at Lanchester town council. It had emerged that some councillors had had talks with a property developer about the possibility of the council selling him some land to build a new housing estate. The only problem was that the land involved was currently a sports field, which included a children's playground.

At first, it was claimed that this was just a rumour, but a local teacher, Mark Burns, who was of the opinion that **there is no smoke without fire**, did a little research and found that talks had indeed taken place. He lived near the proposed development and he and some of his fellow residents decided to start a protest group. 'We're lucky to have heard about this so early,' he said to them. '**Forewarned is forearmed** and we must gather together as much information as possible to fight this development and discuss it with the council.'

'Actions speak louder than words,' said another of the group, Len Waters. 'We need to do more than talk to the council. I think that, for a start, we should stage a protest march through the town. I'm absolutely sure that these talks are at a much more advanced stage than the council have described. A friend of mine's a councillor and, although he didn't actually tell me that talks were well underway, he hinted at it, and a nod is as good as a wink to a blind horse.'

'You could be right. However, there's a long way to go before the sale of the land could be finalized and we needn't rush; more haste, less speed,' said another resident of the area, Peter Frame. 'Gathering information is obviously of prime importance and we should also consult other people. I've heard that there are other groups who are thinking of protesting.'

'If that's true, we should get together with them,' said Mark Burns. 'Union is strength and we'll have much more influence if we belong to a larger group. Let's start telling anyone who might be interested that we are planning a large protest meeting.'

'Good idea and let's hope a lot of people come—the more the merrier,' said Peter Frame. 'A large protest meeting might scare some of the councillors off at an early stage, whereas they might ignore several small groups.'

'United we stand, divided we fall,' agreed Len Waters, 'but I think we should get on with things right away. It's too late to lock the stable door after the horse has bolted and we really don't know what stage the negotiations between the council and the developer are.'

'Let's start by seeing what we can find out about what's going on and by getting as many people as possible to come to a meeting,' said Mark Burns. They all agreed.

Passage 6

Leaving University

45 Blackthorn Street
Barchester
10/6/02

Dear Mum,

This is the second last week of my final university term and so this will be the last letter that I write to you from here. My exams are finished and they seem to have gone all right, but **the proof of the pudding is in the eating** and I won't know how I've done until the results come out next week. On the basis of my previous results, I should do OK, but **nothing is certain but death and taxes**, and it is by no means unknown for someone to do unexpectedly well or badly in university final exams.

I am feeling a bit sad at the idea of leaving university, especially the people. Still, even **the best of friends must part**, and several of us have promised to keep in touch, though I don't know whether or not this will actually happen. **Time will tell**.

I have really enjoyed my time at university, but **all good things must come to an end** and it's time I entered the real world and got a job. Speaking of jobs, I didn't get that one I told you about. **You can't win them all**, I suppose, and, as you know, I was offered one that I turned down. **When one door shuts, another opens** and I've just heard about another one that would suit me even better. I've sent a letter asking for details.

I went shopping for a dress for my graduation ball yesterday and spent much more than I intended. The one that suited me best was much better than the rest and I decided to be extravagant. Then it was **in for a penny, in for a pound** and I decided to buy some rather elegant evening shoes as well. To make my bank account even worse, I then couldn't resist a lovely, but expensive, evening bag. It was a definite case of **one might as well be hanged for a sheep as a lamb**. I don't usually have so much money left at the end of term, but I have been studying hard this term and not going out much.

I've been asked to the ball by one of the final year science students. I don't know him very well, but he seems very nice. He's very quiet, but I suspect that **still waters run deep**. You'll probably meet him at the graduation ceremony before the ball.

I've booked you and Dad in at a nice hotel. It's central and not too expensive. I haven't got the details with me, but I'll email them to Dad at his office.

Look forward to seeing you,

Lots of love,

Jan

Passage 7

Workplace Nerves

The workforce of Martins were feeling extremely nervous. The firm, which manufactured kitchenware, was still privately owned by the Martin family, but recently there had been rumours of a takeover bid. Now, the workers had just heard that Ernest Martin, the managing director, was taking early retirement and had been replaced by a much younger man who had previously worked for one of their major competitors.

'Whether or not there's a takeover,' said Ben Lawrence, 'the new man is bound to make changes. **A new broom sweeps clean**. For a start, he'll almost certainly make some alterations in the production system.'

'The production system has been in need of radical change for years. I think the new man will be more likely to introduce a completely new system than to try to make improvements to the present one. **You can't put new wine in old bottles**,' replied Fred Masters.

'I quite agree,' said Joe Brown. 'I would have thought that he would computerize the whole production system. Most of our competitors have already done so.'

'Well, I'll be out of here if he does,' said Ben Lawrence. '**You**

can't teach old dogs new tricks and I know nothing whatsoever about computers. I'll have no choice but to leave.'

'That's absolute nonsense,' replied Joe Brown. '**You are never too old to learn** and they would most likely send everyone on training courses to learn the new system. They won't want to lose skilled workers.'

'Joe's right,' said Larry Bennett. 'I'm not too keen on the idea of computers either, but **times change and we with time**. If we don't change, we get left behind and the firm can't afford to do that.'

'I think you should all stop worrying about change until we see what happens. **Don't cross the bridge till you come to it**,' said Pete Jenkins. 'In any case, **no news is good news** and the new boss might leave things as they are, for a while at least.'

'That's exactly what I think,' said Alan Black. '**Never trouble trouble until trouble troubles you**. We'll know soon enough if there are going to be changes which will affect us.'

'That's true,' said Larry, 'and **give credit where credit is due** The board of Martins has always been very good about keeping us informed. We can't complain about lack of communication.'

'That may have been true in the past, but the new MD may have a different attitude. I think we should go and ask him what's going on,' said Ben.

'I disagree,' said Larry. '**Let sleeping dogs lie**, and let's wait and see what happens.'

The others decided to follow his advice, but many of them remained nervous.

Passage 8

Holiday Departure

The Jackson family were getting ready to go on holiday and were all busy finalizing their packing and getting in each other's way.

'You'll just forget something if you rush about like that,' said Mr Jackson. '**More haste, less speed**.'

'If a certain person had not spent such a long time in the bathroom, I wouldn't be in such a rush,' said Harry, the elder of the two Jackson sons, looking at his sister Celia. 'I had to wait ages to have a shower.'

'I hope you're not referring to me,' said Celia. 'I just had a quick shower and put on my make-up.'

'**If the cap fits**,' replied Harry. 'In any case, it always takes you hours to put on your make-up, although I don't know why you bother. It doesn't make you look any better.'

'Stop teasing your sister,' said Mr Jackson. 'I thought you might have learned some common sense now that you have been away at college.'

'That's not very likely,' said Rose, the elder of the Jackson girls. '**The leopard does not change his spots**. Harry's been teasing both Celia and me since we were little girls.'

'He's just like your father,' commented Mrs Jackson. 'It's a case of **what's bred in the bone**. Your aunts are always complaining about your father's teasing.'

Mr Jackson decided that it was time to change the subject and said that he would just check to see that all the tickets and holiday arrangements were in order, but his wife said, 'No need. I'm just doing that. **Too many cooks spoil the broth**. We'll just get in a muddle if we both do it.'

Colin, the younger son, said, 'I'll phone for a taxi to go to the airport, shall I? They usually come quite promptly, but **there is always a first time**.'

His father said, 'I've already booked one. It will be here in an hour.'

'That's much too early,' complained Rose. 'I hate hanging around airports.'

'**The early bird catches the worm**,' replied her father, 'and we want to be able to get seats together on the aircraft. It will be a busy flight. Also, we don't know what the traffic will be like at this time of day. It should be quite quiet, but **the unexpected always happens**.'

Rose's brothers and sister started to agree with her, but her father said firmly, '**He who pays the piper calls the tune**. Your mother and I are paying for this holiday and we want to be at the airport in plenty of time.'

Mr Jackson was right about unexpected delays. Their taxi was held up by a road accident, but they got to the airport in time.

'**All's well that ends well**,' said Mrs Jackson thankfully.

Passage 9

Dog Drama

Ellie was feeling miserable and anxious. She had left the garden gate open and her pet spaniel, Spot, had run out on to the road and been hit by a car. The dog had got up and walked away and seemed to be fine, but Ellie wondered if she should take him to the vet.

'**Two heads are better than one**,' she said to herself and phoned her neighbour to ask for advice. Pam from next door came over immediately. She had owned several dogs and Ellie trusted her judgement.

Pam was concerned to see Ellie in such a state. 'Don't blame yourself,' she said. '**Accidents will happen**. Of course, you shouldn't have left the gate open, but **it's easy to be wise after the event** and Spot has never run out before. He seems OK, as far as I can tell, but **it's best to be on the safe side** and I think you should take him to the vet, in case he's been injured internally. **Better be safe than sorry**. I'll come with you.'

Ellie agreed with Pam and they both set off for the vet. A new, larger, more modern veterinary practice had opened in the area, but Ellie's father had advised, '**Don't change horses in mid-stream**,' when she had thought about switching vets. 'Your present vet may be getting old, but he knows the dog well and that counts for a lot. **Better the devil you know than the devil you don't know**.'

On the way to the vet, Ellie was very upset and was still blaming herself. '**What's done cannot be undone**,' said Pam, 'and the dog's probably going to be all right. **Don't meet trouble halfway**.'

When they reached the vet, he examined the dog and was able to reassure Ellie. 'I can't find anything wrong with him. He looks fine and healthy to me. I could do some tests, but I think, at this stage it's best to **leave well alone**. Watch him carefully over the next 24 hours. Make sure that he's eating and drinking properly and try to keep him as quiet as possible. If you're in any way worried, don't hesitate to call me.'

Ellie was enormously relieved and thanked the vet profusely. She was extremely glad that she had gone to see him and was grateful to Pam for going with her. Gradually she began to feel a little less nervous and upset, but she didn't fully recover until after the 24 hours were up and Spot could be assumed to be all right. She never again forgot to shut the gate.

Passage 10

A Moral Dilemma

Mark and Lucy's parents were on holiday and they had decided to have a party. As Mark said, '**When the cat's away, the mice will play**.' It had been their original intention to ask just a few friends each, but **the road to hell is paved with good intentions** and, somehow, invited guests asked uninvited friends and they ended up with a huge number of people. Eventually, the whole thing had got out of control.

Now they were trying to clear up after the party and some of their friends had come round to help. They had expected more volunteers to assist with the clearing-up operation, but it was a case of **a friend in need is a friend indeed**. A surprising number of friends had other things which required their attention.

One of them, Ned, tried to stop Lucy from throwing some of the previous night's food into rubbish bags, saying, '**Waste not, want not**. I'll have some of that.'

'That's cold pizza, Ned, but you'll eat anything,' said Lucy. 'They say that **you are what you eat**, Ned. You should start watching your diet.'

'Stop arguing, you two,' said Mark. 'We have a problem. Jack broke one of Mum's vases last night and we don't know whether to tell her or not. Ken says that he knows someone who will be able to repair it so that it looks as good as new. Maybe it would be best not to say anything about it and hope she won't notice.'

'I think you should tell her,' said Molly. '**Honesty is the best policy** and she might find out anyway. Then she would be very annoyed.'

'I'm more inclined to think that **what the eye doesn't see, the heart doesn't grieve over**,' said Mary. 'If the repair can be as good as you say, then I don't see the point of telling your mother. It's one of those occasions when **silence is golden**, I think.'

'I quite agree,' said Tom. '**Ignorance is bliss**, in my opinion. If you're fairly sure that your mum won't find out, I wouldn't mention it. There's no point in worrying her unnecessarily.'

'**Least said, soonest mended** is what I think—no pun intended,' said Alex. 'Besides, if you mention the broken vase to your mother, she might want to know more about the party, and that's not a good idea.'

'The whole thing's too complicated and we're all too tired to make a decision,' said Lucy. 'Let's wait and see how good the repair is and then we'll decide. **Sufficient unto the day**. Now I think we all need some sleep.'

Passage 11

Travel Broadens the Mind

They say that **travel broadens the mind**. More and more young people are finding out the truth of that for themselves by taking a year off between school and university in order to travel abroad. For some, the travel will be holiday, but others will work in order to fund their holiday. Some will stay in one country, but others will think that **the grass is always greener on the other side of the fence** and keep going from country to country.

Most of the young travellers find that they love travelling. Some even seem to forget all about home and omit to keep in touch with their parents. It may be a case of **out of sight, out of mind** for them, but this is not so for the parents, who worry if they do not hear from their offspring. So, all you young travellers, remember to send the odd postcard to let your family know that you are all right.

The exception proves the rule and a minority of young people find out fairly soon that travel is not for them and decide to return home. They regard the benefits of travel as having been over-rated and come to the conclusion that **east, west, home's best**. For them **there's no place like home** and they intend to stay there.

Many teachers think that taking time out to travel is a good thing for young people. They say that **experience is the best teacher** and travel offers young people a wide range of life experiences. They find that many of the young travellers are made more mature, more independent, and more resourceful by the experience of travel. Frequently, they have to deal with the unexpected and learn that **you never know what you can do until you try**.

Young travellers can take steps to ensure that they encounter as few problems as possible. First of all, they must be careful how they behave. **When in Rome, do as the Romans do** and it is important not to offend people of other countries by behaving in a way that is not acceptable there.

It is also important for young people to have some basic knowledge of the laws of the land in which they are travelling. In most countries, it is the case that **ignorance of the law is no excuse**, and someone who breaks a law will be charged with breaking it, even if they claim that they were totally unaware of the law's existence.

Of course, some young people have unfortunate experiences abroad. However, most of them return home safe and well, full of stories of their adventures, and having had unforgettable experiences.

Passage 12

Inexperienced Climbers

There is growing concern about the number of accidents that are taking place in the mountains in this area. Mountain rescue resources are already stretched to the utmost limit.

Experts say that a large part of the problem is caused by inexperienced climbers. One of them, George Jones, said yesterday, 'There is an increased interest in climbing, which is a good thing, but people are forgetting that **we must learn to walk before we can run**. Some climbers are too ambitious and take unnecessary risks, but in the mountains **discretion is the better part of valour**.'

His colleague, Mark Johnson, commented, 'I quite agree. When learning to climb, people should try not to hurry. They should start with the easier slopes and then gradually progress to harder ones. Also, they should take into consideration the weather conditions here, which can be very changeable. Climbers who know these mountains well always **hope for the best and prepare for the worst**. The sun can be shining one minute, and it can be snowing or blowing a gale the next.'

Harry Martin, a mountain guide, said, 'People who are learning to climb should start off climbing with someone who is really experienced. There are many books on the subject but **example is better than precept**. You learn climbing as you do it, not from books. **A little knowledge is a dangerous thing** and I have known young climbers arrive here thinking that they know all there is to know about climbing after reading a few books. The other day one of them tried to teach me my job and I had to say to him, "**Don't teach your grandmother to suck eggs**." He wasn't very pleased.'

Harry continued, 'I met a group the other day who claimed to have an experienced leader, but he knew very little more than the rest of them, who were totally inexperienced, and he very nearly led them off the edge of a cliff. As the old proverb has it, **if the blind lead the blind, both shall fall into the ditch**.'

'It's also important that they are properly equipped for the local conditions and this need not cost a lot of money,' said Mark. '**A fool and his money are soon parted** and you would be surprised how many people spend a fortune on extremely expensive, state-of-the-art equipment which they will never use, and forget to buy something simple like a compass or a torch.'

'Sometimes it's no bad thing for climbers to have at least a minor fright on the mountains early on their climbing careers,' said George. 'It makes them show more respect for the mountains in the future. **A burnt child dreads the fire** and that attitude means less work for the mountain rescue people.'

Passage 13

A Series of Misfortunes

16 Park Avenue
Monkston
MN12 8JB
3/6/02

Dear Mary,

I hope it's true that **a trouble shared is a trouble halved** because I have a lot of troubles to share with you! I am having a real run of bad luck.

It all started last week when my car was vandalized outside my flat. The damage wasn't too bad and I got it repaired remarkably quickly. Then guess what? The same thing happened again. So it's simply not true that **lightning never strikes twice in the same place**. What is true, as I know to my cost, is that **misfortunes never come singly**.

Just after I discovered what had happened to my car the second time, I discovered that my washing machine had broken down and it cost a great deal of money to have it repaired. **It never rains but it pours**, and the next thing to break down was my fridge freezer. The weather here just now is unusually hot and a fridge is an absolute must. Of course, I had just filled the freezer and I didn't discover that the fridge freezer had gone wrong until all the food was spoiled!

I can't possibly afford to get it repaired and, in any case, I think it probably needs to be replaced. I paid a deposit on a holiday and I am completely broke. I cannot afford to do anything or go anywhere. They say that **the best things in life are free**, but they are lying! **Money isn't everything**, but it certainly adds to the comfort of life.

My catalogue of disasters is not finished! I thought that I might improve my financial position permanently by getting a pay rise. When I started seven months ago, they said that they would review my salary in six months and they haven't. **The labourer is worthy of his hire** and I don't see why I'm paid less than other people doing the same job. However, the boss said no and told me that I am still on probation, which is worrying.

Then I decided to ask my father for a loan, but he reminded me that I had borrowed money from him the year before and hadn't kept my promise to pay it back within three months. He said that it was a case of **once bitten, twice shy** and he wasn't going to lend me any more.

I've heard that **it is better to be born lucky than rich**, but I seem to have been born both unlucky and poor. It doesn't seem right!

I'm sorry to moan on at you, but most of my other friends are on holiday just now and I've no one to talk to. The ones that are here seem to have deserted me, probably because I am acting so miserably. **Laugh and the world laughs with you; weep and you weep alone**, as they say.

I will write again when I'm feeling more cheerful.

Love,

Jane

Exercises on Proverbs

Exercise 1

Complete the following proverbs by inserting the missing word in each.

1 Nothing is certain but ________________ and taxes.

2 A house ________________ cannot stand.

3 Virtue is its own ________________ .

4 Don't change ________________ in mid-stream.

5 Sow the wind and ________________ the whirlwind.

6 Every man has his ________________ .

7 Well begun is ________________ done.

8 What's sauce for the goose is sauce for the ____________ .

9 You cannot get ________________ from a stone.

10 Procrastination is the ________________ of time.

Exercise 2

Complete the following sentences by inserting the missing word in each proverb.

1 Certainly, you may bring a friend to the party; **the more the** ________________ .

2 You should tell your parents that it was you who broke the vase; **confession is** ________________ **for the soul**.

3 Jean was disappointed when Kate chose Alice to be her bridesmaid instead of her, but Alice is Kate's cousin and **blood is thicker than** ________________ .

4 Jack is a lazy young man and I'm not a bit surprised to hear that he is Ken's son. Ken has not done a day's work in his life and **the apple never falls far from the** ________________ .

5 **Love makes the ________________ go round** and there have been a record number of weddings in the local church this year.

6 Some of the other students teased Tom for spending so much time studying, but he passed his exams with top marks and most of them barely obtained pass marks; **he who laughs ________________, laughs longest**.

7 I don't know why Lucy is cleaning the windows when a window-cleaner comes regularly; **why keep a dog and ________________ yourself?**

8 There's a mist coming down on the mountain and we must stay together; **there is safety in ________________** .

9 I was amazed that such a plain child as Elsie had been had grown into such a beautiful young woman, but **seeing is ________________** .

10 It seems to be true that **he travels ________________ who travels alone**; Peter is the only one of us who has no wife or children and he has had by far the most successful career.

Exercise 3

Complete each of the following sentences by inserting from the list of proverbs given after the sentence the proverb which is most appropriate in the context.

1 The traffic is very heavy tonight and we're going to be late for the party; still, ________________ .
(absence makes the heart grow fonder; better late than never; better be safe than sorry; needs must when the Devil drives)

2 As a family, we didn't have much money, but ________________ and we had plenty of good plain food, decent clothes to wear, the sea air and lots of love.
(money talks; charity begins at home; the best things in life are free; hope springs eternal)

3 We have had a very enjoyable trip to the islands, but we have to go home tomorrow; ________________ .
(travel broadens the mind; home is where the heart is; all good things come to an end; something is better than nothing)

4 ________________; try and relax because you're very probably worrying unnecessarily.
(Don't count your chickens before they are hatched; Let sleeping dogs lie; Never trouble trouble until trouble troubles you; You never know what you can do until you try)

5 Grandfather still gets up at 6 am every morning, although he's retired and no longer has to catch an early train into town; ________________ .
(you are never too old to learn; old habits die hard; the early bird catches the worm; there's no fool like an old fool)

6 You should try to do a little studying every evening throughout the term, rather than study all night during the week before the exam; ________________ .
(slow but sure wins the race; delays are dangerous; practice makes perfect; the early bird catches the worm)

7 Anna is of the opinion that ________________ and has decided that it would be better for John not to know that she went out with someone else while he was away in case he gets unnecessarily upset.
(all's fair in love and war; what you don't know can't hurt you; you cannot have your cake and eat it; curiosity killed the cat)

8 If we have any more volunteers working on this project, we'll just get in each other's way and cause confusion;

________________ .

(many hands make light work; the more the merrier; too many cooks spoil the broth; cut your coat according to your cloth)

9 Meg has only herself to blame for the fact that she's in financial difficulties, because she is extremely extravagant and doesn't try to manage her money; ________________ .

(waste not, want not; if the cap fits, wear it; as you sow, so you reap; money is the root of all evil)

10 After the day that I've had I can vouch for the fact that __________________; the train I take to work was cancelled, meaning that I had to run to catch a bus which then broke down, leaving us to wait for another one just as the rain, which wasn't forecast, began pouring down.
(accidents will happen; misfortunes never come singly; lightning never strikes twice in the same place; it's no use crying over spilt milk)

Exercise 4

Complete each of the following sentences by inserting from the list of proverbs given after the sentence the proverb which is most appropriate in the context.

1 Ben has increased the mortgage on his house, relying on the fact that he expects to get a large salary increase, but __________________ and the company is not doing very well just now.
(a miss is as good as a mile; the more you get, the more you want; there's many a slip 'twixt cup and lip; you cannot get blood from a stone)

2 Mary was expecting an invitation to a party and kept running to the window to see if the postman was coming until her mother said, '__________________.'
(No news is good news; A watched pot never boils; Don't cross the bridge till you come to it; Rome wasn't built in a day)

3 Harry said that he refused to join in the gossip about Tom being a thief, but Sally said, '__________________.'
(Silence is golden; No smoke without fire; Don't wash your dirty linen in public; A drowning man will clutch at a straw)

4 Jane apologized for the fact that she could make only a small contribution to the charity appeal, but the organizer said, '__________________.'

(Every little helps; Money isn't everything; The best things come in small packages; It is better to give than to receive)

5 The offer is a very generous one and you should accept it right away; ________________ .
(nothing succeeds like success; when one door closes, another opens; strike while the iron is hot; look before you leap)

6 This is a very difficult situation, but we can survive it, if we cooperate with each other and help each other out;
________________ .
(every man for himself; fair exchange is no robbery; one good turn deserves another; you scratch my back and I'll scratch yours)

7 The boss did not appreciate how much his secretary helped him until she resigned; ________________ .
(you never miss the water till the well runs dry; absence makes the heart grow fonder; you are never too old to learn; it is easy to be wise after the event)

8 You really should discipline the children when they are rude or naughty if you want them to grow into well-behaved adults; ________________ .
(children should be seen and not heard; virtue is its own reward; boys will be boys; spare the rod and spoil the child)

9 The war lasted for quite a few months, but, fortunately, ________________ and we are now enjoying a period of peace.
(the darkest hour is just before the dawn; after a storm comes a calm; everything has an end; what you lose on the swings you gain on the roundabouts)

10 We have just enough money to live on after we've paid the rent, but ________________ and we're very happy.
(moderation in all things; enough is as good as a feast; half a loaf is better than no bread; hunger is the best sauce)

Exercise 5

Write down a proverb which is similar in meaning to each of the following proverbs.

1 Absence makes the heart grow fonder.

2 Give the Devil his due.

3 Fine words butter no parsnips.

4 Fine feathers make fine birds.

5 Once bitten, twice shy.

6 Walls have ears.

7 Every cloud has a silver lining.

8 An old poacher makes the best gamekeeper.

9 Necessity is the mother of invention.

10 You cannot have your cake and eat it.

Exercise 6

Write down a proverb which is similar in meaning to each of the following proverbs.

1 You scratch my back and I'll scratch yours.

2 Ignorance is bliss.

3 He who fights and runs away, may live to fight another day.

4 First catch your hare.

5 One might as well be hanged for a sheep as a lamb.

6 Four eyes see more than two.

7 What you've never had, you never miss.

8 Let sleeping dogs lie.

9 A change is as good as a rest.

10 Let the cobbler stick to his last.

Exercise 7

Write down a proverb which is opposite in meaning to each of the following proverbs.

1 Misfortunes never come singly.

2 Look before you leap.

3 Many hands make light work.

4 Absence makes the heart grow fonder.

5 You are never too old to learn.

6 Opportunity never knocks twice.

7 East, west, home's best.

8 Example is better than precept.

9 Better the devil you know than the devil you don't.

10 Money isn't everything.

Exercise 8

1 The proverb **Don't wash your dirty linen in public** is said to have been derived from a French proverb. Who is said to have popularized this French proverb?

2 **All's well that ends well** is the name of a play as well as a proverb. Who wrote the play?

3 What is the title of the song from which the proverb **There's no place like home** is derived?

4 What was the earlier alternative form of the proverb **Possession is nine points of the law**?

5 What was the original form of the proverb **A rolling stone gathers no moss**?

6 Which saint is credited with making a reply which is the origin of the proverb **When in Rome, do as the Roman do**?

7 From which Shakespeare play does the proverb **A rose by any other name would smell as sweet** come?

8 **You cannot get blood out of a turnip** is an old proverb which still exists in an alternative form. What is this common alternative form?

9 What is another version of the proverb **The eyes are the window of the soul**?

10 What is the origin of the proverb **Good wine needs no bush**?

Exercise 9

1 What is the longer, now less common, version of **To err is human**?

2 What is the name of the Old Testament prophet who is responsible for the proverb **The leopard does not change his spots**?

3 **Love is blind** is a common proverb. What is the name of the Roman god of love who is sometimes represented in sculpture or paintings with a blindfold on?

4 What is the origin of the proverb **Make hay while the sun shines**?

5 What is the earlier form of the proverb **A little knowledge is a dangerous thing** and from which essayist is this quotation?

6 What was the original form of the modern proverb **A miss is as good as a mile**?

7 'He that spareth his rod, hateth his son' is a biblical proverb. What is its modern equivalent?

8 To what kind of cap does the proverb **If the cap fits, wear it** refer?

9 An early form of the proverb **Children should be seen and not heard** referred to females only. What was this proverb?

10 The original form of the proverb **Confession is good for the soul** contained another word. What is this word?

Exercise 10

1 The proverb **Look before you leap** is thought to have its origin in one of Aesop's fables. Which animals are involved in the fable?

2 What is the longer form of the proverb **Ignorance is bliss** and what is the name of the poet from whose poems this is derived?

3 What is the longer, and earlier, form of the proverb **Needs must when the Devil drives**?

4 If **silence is golden**, of what metal is speech?

5 **Slow but sure wins the race** has its origin in one of Aesop's fables. Which animal wins the race in the fable?

6 The proverb **Don't spoil the ship for a ha'porth of tar** sounds as though it is nautical in origin, but it is not. Explain the true origin.

7 The work of which worker has given rise to the proverb **Strike while the iron is hot**?

8 **One swallow does not make a summer** is said to have its origin in an ancient Greek proverb, except that a different season of the year is involved. Which season?

9 What is the Latin proverb from which **Time flies** is derived?

10 The proverb **No man can serve two masters** is biblical in origin. Who were the two masters involved in the original statement?

Index

by topic or concept

Answers

Exercise 1

1 Nothing is certain but **death** and taxes.
2 A house **divided** cannot stand.
3 Virtue is its own **reward**.
4 Don't change **horses** in mid-stream.
5 Sow the wind and **reap** the whirlwind.
6 Every man has his **price**.
7 Well begun is **half** done.
8 What's sauce for the goose is sauce for the **gander**.
9 You cannot get **blood** from a stone.
10 Procrastination is the **thief** of time.

Exercise 2

1 Certainly, you may bring a friend to the party; the more the **merrier**.
2 You should tell your parents that it was you who broke the vase; confession is **good** for the soul.
3 Jean was disappointed when Kate chose Alice to be her bridesmaid instead of her, but Alice is Kate's cousin and blood is thicker than **water**.
4 Jack is a lazy young man and I'm not a bit surprised to hear that he is Ken's son. Ken has not done a day's work in his life and the apple never falls far from the **tree**.
5 Love makes the **world** go round and there have been a record number of weddings in the local church this year.
6 Some of the other students teased Tom for spending so much time studying, but he passed his exams with top marks and most of them barely obtained pass marks; he who laughs **last**, laughs longest.
7 I don't know why Lucy is cleaning the windows when a window-cleaner comes regularly; why keep a dog and **bark** yourself?
8 There's a mist coming down on the mountain and we must stay together; there is safety in **numbers**.
9 I was amazed that such a plain child as Elsie had been had grown into such a beautiful young woman, but seeing is **believing**.
10 It seems to be true that he travels **fastest** who travels alone; Peter is the only one of us who has no wife or children and he has had by far the most successful career.

Exercise 3

1 better late than never
2 the best things in life are free
3 all good things come to an end
4 Never trouble trouble until trouble troubles you
5 old habits die hard
6 slow but sure wins the race
7 what you don't know can't hurt you
8 too many cooks spoil the broth
9 as you sow, so you reap
10 misfortunes never come singly

Exercise 4

1 there's many a slip 'twixt cup and lip
2 A watched pot never boils
3 No smoke without fire
4 Every little helps
5 strike while the iron is hot
6 you scratch my back and I'll scratch yours
7 you never miss the water till the well runs dry
8 spare the rod and spoil the child
9 after a storm comes a calm
10 enough is as good as a feast

Exercise 5

1 Distance lends enchantment to the view.
2 Give credit where credit is due.
3 Actions speak louder than words.
4 Clothes make the man.
5 A burnt child dreads the fire.
6 Little pitchers have big ears.
7 It's an ill wind that blows nobody any good.
8 Set a thief to catch a thief.
9 Needs must when the Devil drives.
10 You cannot have it both ways.

Exercise 6

1 One good turn deserves another.
2 What the eye doesn't see, the heart doesn't grieve over.
3 Discretion is the better part of valour.
4 Don't count your chickens before they are hatched.
5 In for a penny, in for a pound.
6 Two heads are better than one.
7 You cannot lose what you never had.
8 Leave well alone.
9 Variety is the spice of life.
10 Every man to his trade.

Exercise 7

1 Lightning never strikes twice in the same place.
2 He who hesitates is lost.
3 Too many cooks spoil the broth.
4 Out of sight, out of mind.
5 You cannot teach an old dog new tricks.
6 When one door shuts, another opens.
7 Travel broadens the mind.
8 Do as I say, not as I do.
9 Familiarity breeds contempt.
10 Money talks / Money is power.

Exercise 8

1 Napoleon Bonaparte.
2 William Shakespeare.
3 'Home Sweet Home'.
4 Possession is eleven points of the law.
5 The rolling stone gathers no seaweed.
6 St Ambrose.
7 *Romeo and Juliet.*
8 You cannot get blood from a stone.
9 The eyes are the windows of the heart.
10 Formerly shops had a sign outside them to advertise the kind of goods that they sold. In the case of wine shops it was originally an ivy bush, since the ivy, in ancient times, was sacred to Bacchus, the god of wine in Greek mythology.

Exercise 9

1 To err is human; to forgive, divine.
2 Jeremiah.
3 Cupid.
4 Farmworkers had to work as hard and as long as possible on a fine day when the hay was being gathered in, because, if rain came, and prevented further work, the crop might be ruined.
5 A little learning is a dangerous thing; Alexander Pope.
6 An inch in a miss is as good as an ell.
7 Spare the rod and spoil the child.
8 A dunce's cap.
9 A maid should be seen and not heard.
10 The word 'open'.

Exercise 10

1 A fox and a goat.
2 Where ignorance is bliss, 'tis folly to be wise; Thomas Gray.
3 One needs must go when the Devil drives.
4 Silver.
5 The tortoise.
6 The proverb is agricultural in origin. The word 'sheep' is pronounced 'ship' in some English dialects and tar was used on sores and wounds on sheep to prevent flies from landing on them and causing further infection. The idea behind the proverb is that the application of a little tar, which would cost very little time or money, would save the sheep's life. In time, the word 'sheep' came to be spelt 'ship' and the proverb was assumed to have a nautical origin, since tar was also used to preserve and repair the surface of ships.
7 The blacksmith.
8 Spring.
9 *Tempus fugit.*
10 God and Mammon.